I0820414

BIG IDEAS FROM SCIENCE

Published in 2025 by The School of Life
First published in the USA in 2025
930 High Road, London, N12 9RT

Illustrations © Anna Doherty
Designed and typeset by Studio Katie Kerr
Printed in China by Leo Paper Group

A proportion of this book has appeared online at www.theschooloflife.com/articles

Every effort has been made to contact the copyright holders of the material reproduced in this book. If any have been inadvertently overlooked, the publisher will be pleased to make restitution at the earliest opportunity.

The School of Life publishes a range of books on essential topics in psychological and emotional life, including relationships, parenting, friendship, careers and fulfilment. The aim is always to help us to understand ourselves better – and thereby to grow calmer, less confused and more purposeful. Discover our full range of titles, including books for children, here: www.theschooloflife.com/books

The School of Life also offers a comprehensive therapy service, which complements, and draws upon, our published works: www.theschooloflife.com/therapy

www.theschooloflife.com

ISBN 978-1-916753-12-9

10 9 8 7 6 5 4 3 2 1

HOW SCIENTIFIC DISCOVERIES SHAPE OUR LIVES

BIG IDEAS FROM SCIENCE

THE SCHOOL OF LIFE PRESS

THIS BOOK OF

BIG IDEAS

BELONGS TO:

....

INSIDE THIS BOOK ...

A TIMELINE OF SCIENCE

SCIENCE AND YOU

What Is Science, Actually?

That's a pretty huge question! And science is a pretty huge thing. It is divided into lots of different parts. Biology covers the natural world, chemistry deals with what things are made of and physics is all about how everything works (and why).

But we're not just talking about the amazing individual scientific breakthroughs that have changed the way we live – like the astonishing discovery that water, which is a liquid, is actually made up of two gases: hydrogen and oxygen; or the invention of X-rays that can see what is going on inside your body, taking pictures of your bones even though they are covered by your skin. No, we want to think about science as a whole.

So, what's the whole, big idea of science?

Imagine you are living 800,000 to 300,000 years ago, when humans were just evolving and before people knew anything at all about science. What might it have been like? Everything is completely mysterious: what are the stars you see at night? Why does the Moon change shape? What are rainbows? And what about lightning – where does it come from?

Every culture tells fascinating stories about all these things. The stars, some say, are the eyes of people watching you from the sky; the Sun is angry with the Moon and cuts away at it until there's only a tiny bit left, and then it grows again; a rainbow is a bridge to another, wonderful world and, when lightning strikes a tree next to your camp or village, they say it's because a god in the mountains is angry with you.

Before there was science, people *believed* myths like these. They didn't think *we have no idea what lightning is so let's just make up a story*. They looked at the available evidence they had and became *convinced* that lightning was being thrown at them by someone immensely powerful – and very angry.

So, based on this evidence, they might try to *control* what was happening by doing special dances or offering gifts that they hoped would please and calm down the beings firing flashes of light at them. And when it didn't work, they'd think, *maybe we aren't doing the dance the right way or maybe we gave the wrong gifts*.

Eventually people worked out that the stars are actually massive balls of hot gas that are more than 40 trillion kilometres away and they certainly aren't looking at you or anyone else. The Moon is a large lump of rock that is orbiting the Earth, and both are moving around the Sun. Sunlight hits the Moon at different angles at different times, and the Moon reflects that light. As the Moon's position changes during its orbit, it appears to change shape, creating the different phases of the Moon that we can observe. Rainbows are caused by sunlight passing through drops of water and you can't even touch them, let alone walk over them to another world.

The process of gradually moving away from myths and finding out how things work and what is really going on is called science. This is what all the people with their telescopes and microscopes and test tubes are doing: they are trying to find out how things actually work – as opposed to how one might imagine they work.

When you find out what is really going on, it makes the world feel a bit clearer and explains why some ideas don't work. Lightning, really, is electricity. It happens when electrical charges inside clouds build up and are then released. As they head towards the ground, they meet other electrical charges heading the other way, creating a flash of lightning. It's got nothing at all to do with anyone being angry. However amazing the dance or however carefully the gifts are chosen, such things *cannot* stop there being lightning storms.

And it is for the same reason that science leads to amazing technology. Once you understand how things actually work, you can use that knowledge to do amazing things and invent incredible technology.

For instance: do you know how magnets work? People had known for centuries that certain types of rock are natural magnets, but they just had no idea why. They might have thought it was magic. It took an incredibly long time to figure out that magnetism is a force that can pull certain metals towards each other or push them away. Magnets are surrounded by a magnetic field that is stronger at each end (known as poles). The Earth itself is a giant magnet, with a magnetic field that is all around us all the time, though we don't normally notice it. But once those discoveries were made (over many hundreds of years), it was possible to use magnetic fields to send messages, which is how radio and Wi-Fi work.

And people have always known that birds can fly, but it was extremely difficult to understand how they managed it. Many ancient people thought it was because birds were being called up to the gods in the sky. Or maybe because they flapped their wings a lot.

But the real explanation is quite different. What's really going on is that birds are creating a zone of low-pressure air above them; a very clever flapping motion helps them do that, but flapping isn't the secret. The secret is the difference in air pressure below and above. And you can create that same effect without flapping if you have the right shape of wing. This is why we were able to design and build planes with fixed wings.

Myths are lovely stories, and they give us clues as to how our ancestors lived, but they don't often give you accurate information. Science might not always sound as fun, but it does help you find out how things really are – and lets Granny send you a photo of her graduation from flying school!

Why Is Science Important?

So, we've talked about what science is – but this book is not *just* about science because it's *also* about someone very special and very interesting: *you*. It's about how *science* can be important to *you*.

If you ask most grown-ups why science is important, one of the first things they might say is 'because it gives us technology'. Without science, there wouldn't be freezers or microwaves – and your pizza wouldn't be ready in two minutes. Without science, there wouldn't be anaesthetics – and a visit to the dentist to get a filling would be agony. And lots of other things too, of course.

And all that is great. But does it really explain why it's important *to you* to find out about science? Maybe not. After all, *you* don't need to know about science to use technology: you don't need to understand how electricity really works to recharge your phone or use a TV. You just need the people who design TVs or manage the power networks to know what *they* are doing.

So, maybe science is just *interesting*. Science tells you amazing facts, like how an asteroid helped to wipe out the dinosaurs about 66 million years ago, or how there are at least 50,000 different kinds (or species) of spiders – though perhaps, if you're like us, you'd rather *not* know that! Super, but there are billions of interesting things apart from science: history is interesting, sport is interesting, so are films, cooking, drawing, music, parties, keeping a diary and learning to dance ...

Do you need to know a lot about science to get a job or be successful when you are older? Usually not. (Of course, if you are going to be a scientist or a science teacher, you'd better get studying.) But actually, hardly anyone works directly in science. Even if you don't become a scientist, knowing about science will help you in many different jobs and in all aspects of your life.

But there is another important thing about science that people hardly ever talk about – but we really want to and it's why we've written this book. Finding out about science can help you *grow*. We don't mean grow physically – finding out about space and atoms and evolution won't make you taller. But it can help you grow *psychologically*.

What does that mean? It means things that are related to your mind and your emotions: helping you understand your thoughts and feelings, your worries and problems, getting more confident or less anxious. Life can feel pretty tricky and confusing at times, and finding out about science can help you make sense of yourself and other people.

You might wonder: *how can that be?* Science investigates the stars using huge telescopes, it studies how many kinds of insects there are in the Amazon rainforest; science is people in lab coats and protective glasses doing complicated things with chemicals in test tubes. How can that be connected to you and your life? What if you've got (maybe) a friend who's not talking to you? How come Dad is in some ways so nice and in some ways so embarrassing? What if you're not sure what you want to do when you're grown up? How can learning about science possibly help with the things that matter in your day-to-day life?

Good questions! And this book is going to answer them.

You Are a Scientist

Science is an important part of the long, complicated and unfinished story of human civilisation. Slowly, and with difficulty, we move from believing myths to understanding how things work and why things happen.

But in a funny – and important – way, this is just like your own story, too. Like everyone (including us), you've probably grown up believing *myths* – certain things about yourself and the world around you. Maybe not myths about the stars or rainbows, probably. They are more likely to be myths about yourself and other people.

What could they possibly be? On the next page are some examples of everyday myths that can *feel* true. And let's compare them with a more scientific, more accurate and realistic picture, based on actual evidence.

MYTH:	WHAT IS REALLY THE CASE:
If you don't pass the maths test on Wednesday or get asked to the party on Friday – your whole life will be a failure.	*The success of someone's life can basically never be traced back to a single moment. It's very unlikely the test or the party will be decisive.*
Being happy means being famous.	*There are many sources of happiness and fame, in fact, might be an obstacle to happiness.*
If someone is smiling, they must be happy.	*They could be happy if they are smiling, but they could also be pretending or hiding their real feelings.*
If your parents argue, it means they don't love each other.	*There are many reasons why adults argue. It's OK to disagree with someone. If people argue a lot though, it's maybe a sign that they need to work on a particular problem.*
You are supposed to have a pretty clear idea of what you want to do for a job by the age of 12.	*Very often, people who like their work had no idea at all when they were young of what they would be doing as adults*
Adults understand everything and almost always have the answers.	*There are so many different adults and so many different things to understand.*
Adults basically understand nothing and almost never know what's best.	*Most adults understand some important things and no adult understands everything that's important.*

Finding out about science means moving away from the myths you (like all of us) merely feel are true and discovering what's actually the case.

The ideas we happen to believe in today are based on how we interpret the world. The exciting thing is that we can keep learning new things and be ready to change our minds.

A Tricky Thing About Science

Science means trying to find out what is real. And sometimes that's *not* going to be what we'd *like* to hear. How things *actually* are might be very different from how we'd *wish* them to be.

It would be lovely, of course, if ice cream was an ideal and healthy breakfast food, but it's not because it doesn't give you the sustained energy that cereal does.

Or, on a global scale, it would be great if it didn't matter at all how much fossil fuels we burn. Unfortunately, science tells us the opposite.

Fossil fuels are created from ancient trees that fell down long ago and have been buried by mud, rock and stones. Over millions of years the pressure above became greater and greater and this made the trees heat up, slowly turning them into the type of rock that we call 'coal' or a liquid that we call 'oil'. The big thing about coal and oil is that they can burn very easily, and when they burn, they release a lot of energy. We use these materials to produce electricity or fuel. But there is a problem: fossil fuels have a damaging effect on the environment. When you burn fossil fuels, they release a gas into the air called carbon dioxide. This builds up in the atmosphere and slowly increases the temperature of the Earth's atmosphere – what we call the 'greenhouse effect'.

The fear is that getting more scientific and being more realistic means that things might be worse or more difficult than you'd thought.

But there's another story to science: what's real might be *better* than you imagined. So, adopting a more scientific approach to fears or worries could help you overcome them

Imagine a 5-year-old who's frightened of going to bed because they think a lion might be hiding in the wardrobe. Science can be their friend; it can take away their fear. It helps to ask realistic questions: how would the lion get there? A lion's coat makes it hard to spot in the long sun-burnt grass of the African savannah but incredibly easy to see if it is strolling down your street. If the lion is hiding in the cupboard, how did it close the door behind it? A lion's paws didn't evolve to deal with handles. Also, lions have no natural interest in interacting with human beings.

Your mind, like that of a 5-year-old, might worry about things that it's making up. Science, basically, is soothing a fear. It might just show that an anxiety can't be real: quite often, the more you understand about reality, the *less* frightening it becomes.

Or what about an 8-year-old who dreams of becoming a professional football player? What might taking a more scientific view mean to them? Science takes into account numbers: there might be millions of people with similar dreams and only a handful will play at the top level. It may work out for them, but the chances of becoming a professional football player are very low.

That might seem quite negative. But maybe it's not. The *realistic* – more accurate, more scientific – picture is that having a good life has nothing much to do with playing professional football. There are many other things they could turn out to be good at and enjoy. If football is their passion, they could become a coach, a physiotherapist or a sports journalist, or just play football for fun. There are many *different* ways adults can lead interesting and fulfilling lives.

Getting more like a scientist – getting a more accurate picture of how things really are – can tell you things that you don't really want to hear, but it can also be a huge relief.

How Does Science Work?

How does a society – or a growing person like you (or indeed an adult who is still growing psychologically) – move from myth to a better understanding of the world around them? How did science manage to find out so much about what's actually going on? What have scientists been doing all this time?

It's not one thing – it's a whole lot of different things. And what's funny and rather wonderful is that you can do them all as well (no lab coats or telescopes required).

1. SCIENCE STARTS BY ADMITTING 'I DON'T KNOW' AND THEN ADDS 'I WANT TO FIND OUT'.

Remember, long ago, people thought they knew all about lightning (sent from angry gods) and the stars (their ancestors looking down on them). It must have been pretty brave and interesting people who said, 'I'm not so sure, I *wonder* if there's a different explanation'.

Does this ring a bell? Maybe you don't actually know why Dad gets upset sometimes – but sometimes is so nice. Or why people say exams are important – though plenty of grown-ups have done well in life without passing any. Or why a friend suddenly stops talking to you. Or why it's so hard to know what you want to do (or should do) for a job.

Rather than jumping to conclusions based on feelings or saying things like 'most people think ...' science says, 'let's work it out properly'. And it's got no problem with suggesting that most people might be wrong.

It's a very interesting attitude. It means saying: it's actually *good* to realise you don't know something. Normally we admire people who know lots of things already and it can feel a bit embarrassing to admit, *actually, I've no idea*. But science says: that's great! It's only when you say you don't know that you can start to investigate what might really be going on.

Without trying to get to any answers just yet, can you make a little list of things you realise you don't understand, but would like to?

II. SCIENCE IS VERY INTERESTED IN EVIDENCE AND EXPLANATION

Searching for evidence is probably how science got started in the first place. Let's do a bit more of our imaginative time-travelling back to very early human history.

Imagine you are wandering outside the village, and you see what looks like a wolf in the distance. Oh no! Is it planning to attack the village? You run back and tell a parent. They are worried too, but they want to be sure. So, they ask: 'Did you really see it? Could it have been a grey rock?' You take them to the place and there's an animal footprint in the soft earth. That proves it! Maybe. Could it be the print of another animal? No, it's too big to be a fox and too small to be a woolly mammoth. Brilliant. But – how old is the footprint? It could be from weeks ago. No! It's in some mud from the rain early this morning – and it didn't rain for days before that. It must be printed from today. Raise the alarm! There's a wolf nearby. But then you look more closely in the surrounding area. There are other prints, but the spaces between them are uneven. This is the track of a wounded wolf; it was limping badly. And there are drops of blood. No need to panic, it won't attack. Poor thing, it's probably looking for a place to rest.

Think about what's happening. You and your parents are using evidence and logic (that is, clear thinking) to work out what *must actually* have happened. You think hard about the evidence and keep asking, what does it *really* show? It's only after you've asked a fair few questions that you decide, yes, the most obvious explanation is that a lame wolf was here earlier today.

This might not *sound* like science: where are the test tubes and the clever instruments for measuring things? But actually, this is right at the centre of science, because science is all about finding more evidence and working out very carefully what it is most likely to mean.

You could ask, for example, how fast sound travels through the air. Normally, you think that doesn't take any time at all: you are talking to someone, and you don't have any feeling that it's taking *time* for their words to reach you. But what if you look for more evidence? Suppose you go to watch a fireworks display on a beautiful clear evening. You *see* the fireworks shooting up into the sky and then bursting into shimmering light, and *then* about one second later, you *hear* the loud pop of them bursting apart.

This gap is *evidence* that eyesight is faster than hearing; it suggests that light travels a lot faster than sound. If you know the distance precisely and have a very accurate clock, you can then get more evidence about how fast sound actually travels through the air.

This is what an experiment is: it's a way of getting evidence. Science is all about trying things out to find out what happens and thinking about what that means.

For scientists, evidence is really important when they have a clever idea, but no one believes them. One experiment from the 18th century was to do with diamonds. Antoine Lavoisier, a French chemist, believed that diamonds and coal were made of the same element – carbon. Diamonds, obviously, are hugely expensive; they glitter beautifully in the light and are worn in prized jewellery. The evidence of our eyes says nothing could be more different than a dazzling diamond and a boring lump of coal, which is much cheaper and which not many people would choose to place at the centre of an engagement ring. But what happens if you burn a diamond? It turns out it's very similar to what happens if you burn coal – it disintegrates and releases carbon dioxide. (Although it takes a much higher temperature to burn diamonds than coal.)

Lavoisier's experiment provided evidence that diamonds and coal are very closely related. And it provided evidence for a further idea: if coal and diamonds are both made of the element carbon, the difference in how they look could be to do with how that element is arranged.

An experiment, you could say, is a way of asking questions and getting answers. And that's something that can be really useful in everyday life. You ask a lump of coal and a diamond what happens when they burn, and – unexpectedly but importantly – their answers turn out to be quite similar. But in our own lives we don't always ask carefully what the 'evidence' really shows, and we don't try to find more evidence.

Let's look at how this might go on an ordinary Tuesday evening: you want Mum to help you with something and she turns round and says, 'Sorry, I just can't right now'. Understandably, you feel disappointed and think something like, *she's angry with me* or *she's being mean* or *she doesn't care*. But there might be lots of different explanations: maybe she's just had an important call at work. Maybe she's very tired. Maybe later she'll think, *oh I wish I hadn't responded like that*. Maybe she really wishes she had time to help you but has a million things to do right now.

We often jump to quick, emotional conclusions based on how something has made us feel. Science is the opposite of that; it's very careful to check what the other logical explanations could be.

We've listed some common situations and suggested how you might respond to the 'evidence' you come across and what conclusions you could understandably jump to. What we want you to do is think like a scientist. We want you to imagine what other explanations there might be. (By the way, 'X' just means someone – anyone – including, perhaps, you.)

What you think at first may be quite different from what is really going on. And by observing and asking questions, you can find evidence about what might really be happening. Someone could say – for example – that whales are fish; there seems to be plenty of 'evidence'. Whales live in the sea; they have fins and tails, just like fish. But when people – scientists – started to observe whales more closely, they realised this couldn't be true. Whales are actually more closely related to mice than sharks. They don't breathe via gills, like fish, they have lungs, like mammals. They breathe air and are warm-blooded, just like us. Once you look clearly at the details – at the evidence (and this is what science wants you to do) – you realise that what seemed the 'obvious' explanation isn't necessarily the right one.

Logical Explanations for Everyday Situations

SITUATION 1: BIRTHDAY PARTY

EVIDENCE
X didn't invite me to their birthday party.

CONCLUSION I JUMP TO
X doesn't like me.

OTHER POSSIBLE EXPLANATIONS
X can only invite a certain amount of people.
They thought I wouldn't want to come.
They were too shy to ask me.
Their parents don't get on with my dad.
They forgot to ask me.
They quite like me, but not that much.

SITUATION 2: MATHS TEST

EVIDENCE
X failed a maths test.

CONCLUSION I JUMP TO
X is really bad at maths.

OTHER POSSIBLE EXPLANATIONS
They are bad at maths but are really good at lots of other things.
They find maths hard and need extra support.
X wasn't feeling well that day and couldn't focus.

III. SCIENCE IS INTERESTED IN DISAGREEMENT

You might dislike disagreement: it's annoying when other people won't agree with you, and it can be pretty horrible to be around others who are always arguing with each other. But science thinks there can – and should – be really positive, intelligent disagreement. Let's look at an example.

If you look closely at this map of the world, you might notice that the east coast of South America (facing towards Africa) looks like a kind of mirror image of the west coast of Africa (pointing towards South America). Once you observe that, you can *imagine* how they might once have been joined together and somehow pulled apart. And in the early 1900s, a lot of people did start to think that must have happened. To add to their evidence, they pointed out that you could find the same sorts of rocks on each coast, even though they're now separated by the Atlantic Ocean. Good point.

But some people disagreed. Yes, they could see the intriguing shapes of the coasts and they didn't deny that there were similar rocks very far apart. Their point was that they couldn't see *how* two enormous landmasses *could* have moved. They are immensely heavy; they are anchored everywhere to the seabed. No *known* force could possibly budge them. Also a good point!

At this point, the science was incomplete. There were good reasons to think that the continents *must* have moved apart *and* there were good reasons to think that they *couldn't* move. It was completely reasonable to be on either side. It was the *disagreement* that was intelligent and reasonable.

It turned out in the end that the movers were right – but for a reason no one had imagined. In the 1950s, people began to map the depths of the Atlantic Ocean and they found (to their complete surprise) that there were massive volcanoes far below the surface. It was the immense force connected to these eruptions that was – very, very slowly – moving Africa and South America apart. Once this new fact had been discovered and understood, the disagreement was settled. But before that, it was completely sensible that there were two sides, each arguing their case.

What science is saying is that there are things it's entirely understandable to disagree about because we don't yet know enough to fully decide the question. Disagreement needn't just be two people arguing; it can be two or more intelligent and thoughtful people seeing a difficult problem in different ways. The people who turned out to be wrong weren't wrong because they were silly or mean or just too arrogant to listen. They were raising a very sensible objection that needed a scientific answer.

Science is full of examples of extremely clever people getting things wrong. Another huge question, in the past, was: *how old is the Earth*? It's incredibly difficult to know. If you look at a rock, you can guess it's pretty old. But *how old*? Ten thousand years old, ten million, a hundred million? Just looking at it doesn't give you any clue at all.

Up until the early 20th century, even the cleverest, most serious people were totally wrong about how old the Earth is. The problem was this: the

Earth, they correctly reasoned, must be younger than the Sun. So, how old is the Sun? This felt like an easier question to answer. Why? Because the Sun is burning. So, they could ask: *how long can the Sun burn?* If you are burning a lump of coal, it burns longer if it is bigger. So far as anyone could tell at that point, the longest even something as huge as the Sun could possibly burn at such a very high temperature would be around 25 million years. So that's the oldest the Earth could possibly be, and it might be quite a lot less than that (if the Sun isn't about to use up all its fuel).

This answer is amazingly, deeply wrong. The Earth, we now know, is around 4.5 *billion* years old – nearly 200 times older than the clever people of 1900 thought.

The thing was, they were wrong for very intelligent and sensible reasons. It was only in the 20th century that someone explained how the Sun could really be working. It doesn't burn like a huge coal fire at all. Its energy comes from something called nuclear fusion. In stars, nuclear fusion happens when hydrogen atoms are fused together to make helium. This releases lots of energy, which causes extremely high temperatures for billions and billions of years.

It can be hard to understand why people have different ideas to us, but science shows us that people can look at the same situation and come up with completely different ideas. Science shows us that someone can be very reasonable, well-intentioned, clever – and completely wrong.

And when it turns out you were the one who was wrong, you can change your mind, admit you were wrong and still feel proud of yourself.

What we're going to do in a moment is start looking carefully at some of the main moments when scientists took interesting steps in understanding better how things work – and we're going to be talking all the way about how that can help you. What's your equivalent of the step they took? And how can that help you in your life?

But first, there's one more big idea about science we want to talk about.

Who Can like Science?

There's quite a strong temptation to think that science is for people who are good at science tests, people who do really well at maths and who dream (maybe) about working in a laboratory someday. And of course, science is a great thing for them. But it's not *only* for them. In fact, it *mustn't* be only for them. Science is for everyone!

We often have a picture of people following one path. People generally think that if you like one thing then you can't possibly like something else that's very different. You become a scientist and know all about that but you're not going to be a great dancer or wear stylish clothes or write poetry. But equally, if you do love fashion or dancing or poetry, or are terrible at tests, then science can't be for you. Well, we think that's all very silly and unhelpful. Of course one person can like all those things!

We'd like you to get to know Ada Lovelace, who was one of the most significant figures in the development of computer science. Back in the early 19th century, she wrote the first algorithm (instructions that tell a computer how to do something), which is a huge factor in our lives today.

Lovelace, true to her fabulous name, was fantastically glamorous. She loved fashion and was a keen musician. If she were living today, she would probably be going to all the smartest parties in the world. But that wasn't her main thing. Lovelace combined a love for music with being extremely serious and excited about science. She even worked on musical compositions based on numbers.

Think of what that meant. She was showing there didn't need to be a gap between loving science and being interested in music – you could care about both. Unfortunately, not so many people in the world today are convinced about that. They think you go for one or the other. We need more versions of Ada Lovelace to show that's not true.

Or what about the most famous scientist of the 20th century, Albert Einstein? He was always great at maths and physics but terrible at other subjects like languages and had to leave school because he couldn't pass the exams. But that didn't stop him, because what really mattered was that he was very imaginative. He loved music and poetry. He used his imagination to picture what it might be like if you were sitting on a beam of light and travelling with it, and this led him to some amazing discoveries. But the thing we're saying is that it was his imagination, not his ability to pass tests when he was 13 or 16 that made him a great scientist. And that's maybe a bit different from what you'd expect.

So, whether you become a great scientist or not, the really important thing is to be interested in science. It would be great to live in a world where everyone is curious and interested in science. Science just asks the central questions: *what is real? How do things actually work?* And that shouldn't be something only a few people care about.

So even if you don't know what NaCl is (salt), or why $E = mc^2$ (it's one of our friend Einstein's big discoveries), or if being asked to divide 193 by 17 without a calculator makes you quake (it's 11.3529412, but we did use a calculator) ... science can be exciting and important to you. Because it turns out science is really around us all the time, in the background, helping to explain the ideas that matter in your life.

So, we're going to follow the story of science and investigate some key moments when people were discovering big things about how the world really is. And we'll see, at the same time, how what *they* were finding out *then* can help you with what *you* care about *now*.

A TIMELINE OF SCIENCE

We've organised the story of science (and how it can help you in life) by *when* some big science ideas were discovered, starting with the oldest and moving to the most recent. Here's a timeline of what it all looks like.

14:23

Mesopotamia, c. 3000 BCE

The Creation of Bronze

For at least 2.6 million years, all round the world, people have crafted tools. The first tools were made of stone: hammers and, after a lot of careful chipping away at the edges, knives. This was in the long period – lasting for more than 2 million years – known as (did you guess?) the *Stone* Age.

But some stones have a secret. If they get incredibly hot – perhaps when heated with fire – part of them *melts*, leaving behind a very interesting material, a kind of metal we now call copper. When people first found it, it must have seemed almost magical: if you took a lump of it and hit it with your (stone) hammer, you could flatten it; and when heated, you could bend it and shape it.

This new thing – copper – was mysterious. It was *inside* the rock, but if you broke the rock into little pieces, you couldn't find it: you had to heat the rock to a very high temperature. It would give off lots of gas and grey dust and leave a little bit of copper behind. Somehow these rocks seemed to be made of metal and gas and dust. But how could that possibly be? It took thousands of years to fully understand what was happening – but this was a moment when a big science *question* was starting to be asked: *what are things secretly made of?*

While this was happening, other people discovered that if you heated different rocks they would also leave behind metals. In particular, they found another rather soft metal called tin.

Tin and copper can't usually be found in the same places, and it was a long time before people got round to trying an experiment. What happens if you heat some copper *and* some tin *together*? Mostly the results of the mixture were pretty terrible – you just got a lumpy mess. But then they discovered something very odd. It turned out that if you use pretty much exactly nine times as much copper as tin, you get a brand new, and very exciting, metal: bronze.

Bronze was very useful because it was much harder and stronger than copper. You could make very sharp and quite long swords out of it, which would give you a huge advantage over people only using stone weapons. You could use bronze to make things to protect yourself – like a helmet or a shield. However, it was so tricky and difficult to make bronze that only the most important and powerful people could ever hope to possess such marvellous things.

Bronze was lovely because it was easier to melt, and its copper content made it easy to shape. If you polished it, it reflected firelight or the sunlight very beautifully, so it could be shaped into wonderful objects, such as a sacred dragon or a richly decorated cup for religious ceremonies.

But bronze was also immensely puzzling. How could mixing two fairly soft materials result in something harder? And why did you have to get the proportions just right? Why *nine* times as much copper as tin? Why should that matter so much? Again, these were powerful questions – they seemed to be pointing at secret rules working *inside* nature.

This is an important part of how science starts. You realise there *must* be an explanation for something, but you can't as yet work out what the explanation is. You've got *evidence*: the right proportion of copper and tin makes bronze. You know it happens, but you don't know *why* or *how* it happens. So, the next step is trying to work out the answers.

Bronze is the result of two very interesting processes. One is *extraction*: when you find a way of getting a little bit of copper or tin out of a stone by heating it. You find the useful bit hidden inside something else. But making wonderful bronze also requires *combination* – you find out how to put different things together to make something new. And these two processes are also very important in your life, even though you're probably not (we're guessing) involved in metallurgy: the science and business of making metals.

YOU ARE AN EXTRACTOR

You might only need a tiny bit of something. The clever Bronze Age people didn't need the whole rock, only the little bit of copper, or tin, within it. In the same way, a book might just have *one* idea out of many it contains that really helps you; a film might have just one scene that really speaks to you; there might be just one line in a song that makes sense of something that you've been feeling.

But it's not so easy. Our brains tend to say 'I love that song' – you have to ask yourself the extractor question: *what's the little bit I most like*? You have to concentrate on the one or two details that most please you.

You can actually try this with a story or film, or even a person. You don't need to like everything about someone or agree with everything they say to realise that they offer you something important.

YOU ARE A COMBINER

Like the people who made bronze, you put together *different* things and make something new. You put a scarf together with a coat and both look nicer. You like the front of that car and the back of another one – would they work together?

This is also what some artists do. This is a special moment because you are seeing something of your creativity.

What would you like to extract from your favourite songs, books, pictures or films?

What might you combine them with?

Like the Bronze Age people a long time ago, you might need to make many, many experiments to gradually work out which things you need to extract, and which combinations actually result in something that's new and wonderful.

What Size is the Earth?

When you think about it, ordinary experience gives you no clue at all that we are all living on a large ball of rock. Looking out of the window or going for a walk doesn't suggest *anything* much about that. Quite possibly, for thousands and thousands of generations, our prehistoric ancestors didn't even wonder about it at all.

But you can imagine how some people could have become *curious*. After all, you might think, *what's beyond that hill and what's beyond that?* Does it ever come to an end? Does the land and sea just go on *forever?* So, even if you don't know, you can start to think: if the land doesn't go on forever, there must be some shape to where we are? It must be some kind of size.

And so, you can start to ask: well, *what* shape, *what* size? And how could we possibly begin to find out? In the past there was zero chance of travelling far enough, or getting high enough, or digging a hole deep enough to find an answer. But there was one rather brilliant possibility that occurred to a clever scientist called Eratosthenes, who was born in North Africa, in what is now Libya.

He had made an interesting observation when he heard about a deep well in Syene, in the South of Egypt. He noticed that sunlight reached the bottom of a very deep well and glinted off the water far below on one day of the year. It gave him an idea. That must mean that on that day, the Sun was directly overhead.

OK. But what does this prove? How does this help? Greek scholars at the time agreed that the Earth was a sphere, but no one had discovered how big it was.

Eratosthenes had the chance to find out. He was a rather clever man and very good at maths. Knowing that the Earth was a sphere, he realised that he could use geometry (maths) to work out how big it was. Now that he knew the angle of the Sun in Syene on a particular day, if he measured the angle in another place on the same day, he could calculate the size of the Earth. He used Alexandria, also in Egypt but far to the north, because that's where he worked, and because he happened to know how far away from Syene it was, which was also an important part of his calculation.

Our friend probably drew a diagram like this one on the next page. Then, in his diagram, he just continued the curve all the way round to make a circle. And using the distance he already knew, he could work out how far it must be all the way round.

And – wonderfully, but also very logically – he was pretty much right.

It was quite a spectacular discovery. It meant that the Earth was huge in comparison with the parts that he – and people in general – knew about it. The most adventurous travellers he knew had covered only a tiny portion of the whole surface.

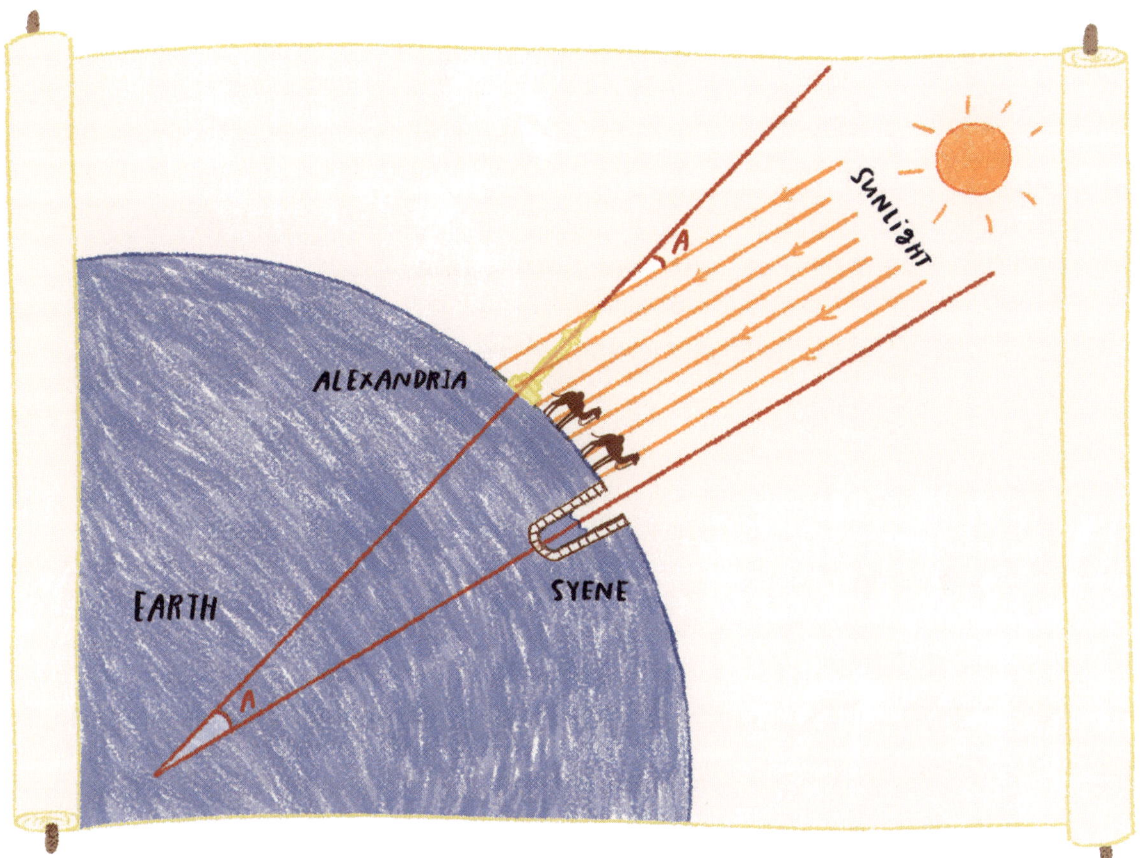

What might be going on across the rest of the globe? Neither he nor anyone else had the slightest idea.

Our friend was super clever, but he lived ages ago – and if we want to find out how big the Earth is, we can just read a book or check online. So, what can he and his ingenious discovery possibly have to say about you and your life?

What Eratosthenes is telling you is something very big and basic. He became interested in wells because he was already curious about the Earth. There was something specific he wanted to understand, and he asked about it wherever he went. In effect, he asked the well: what can *you* tell me about the size of the Earth? He used what he *did* know (that the Earth is a sphere) to make a pretty good guess about something he *didn't* know (how big the Earth is).

And this is a big idea. What do you want to find out about? It might be:

How do I become a better friend?

Why do people argue so much?

How do I get to be the best at something?

So, take a moment (or a week or ten years) to think:

What do you want to understand?

What puzzles you?

What would it really help you to know about better?

These are huge, great questions – and, to be honest, much more important in your life than knowing the shape or size of the Earth.

Like Eratosthenes, you can use what you *already* know to work things out. And you'll find that lots of people have little bits of information to offer. Granny knows something, so does Dad, so does a friend, and so does their mum. They won't know the whole answer – you have to work that out – but they are like the well: they give you clues as best they can.

You become a question-asker and a puzzle-solver, just like Eratosthenes.

Baghdad, around 1200 Years Ago

The Beauty of Mathematics

Let's set the imagination dials for Baghdad, which is today the capital of Iraq, in the 9th century CE. At that time, it was the largest city on the planet and seen as the cultural centre of the world.

As we zoom in, there's something amazing: the city is almost perfectly circular, with four straight main streets leading out from the mosque and palace in the centre to four gates, equally spaced out, in the city walls.

It's a bit like a class in which you are being taught about circumferences and diameters. It looks like a city that was designed in a maths lesson. And that's not an accident: the people who founded it were obsessed with maths.

Why? One big reason was that they realised maths is very important to science and to our understanding of the world, because nature is full of secret patterns that relate to numbers. From the spirals on seashells to the constellations the stars form, maths is all around us. If you count carefully, you realise that the Earth is following a 365.25-day orbit around the Sun, while the Moon takes 27.3 days to orbit the Earth. These numbers mean that sunrise and sunset change throughout the year, but they follow a very precise pattern, as do the seasons and the changing 'phases' of the Moon.

Remember, at this time in history, people still generally thought the world was being governed by the lives and feelings of special people they called gods. The Sun was someone in a chariot speeding through the sky. The Moon was getting thin and then filling out. But if nature follows precise mathematical patterns (and they were finding out that it does), then it can't be the result of the changing moods or whims or emotions of special big people in the sky. There must be laws and rules. The Islamic scientists in Baghdad were starting to realise that the world – the world of objects – follows rules of maths.

Geometry (which is all about creating and measuring shapes) didn't just inspire scientists in Baghdad, though – it also inspired architects and artists who loved maths. That can sound a bit strange today because we tend to suppose that if you like painting or design then you probably will not be much interested in sums and equations.

But Islamic artists used maths to make some of the most beautiful designs in the world – on walls and ceilings, and for making carpets, pottery and illustrations in books.

The designs are all based on simple rules of geometry, using shapes like squares and triangles – as well as more complicated things like pentagons (shapes with five sides) and dodecagons (which have twelve sides). The designers put these shapes together, combining colour and lines to make intricate, delightful patterns.

You can try creating some designs yourself – you might find it makes you feel rather calm and satisfied and less bothered about what happened at school today.

Decorative illustration from a Qur'an manuscript

The designers of the time showed us how maths can inspire art and creativity, and how numbers and patterns are all around us. And in the process, they unlocked a strange secret about beauty. Today, nobody ever really asks, *what makes something beautiful?* People like things for their own reasons.

But the Islamic designers had some very specific ideas about beauty: they felt that maths could create beauty because things are simple *and* complicated *at the same time*. From a distance, the basic pattern of an Islamic design feels quite obvious. There's a clear structure. But if you concentrate on the details, it feels more and more complicated.

The blue tiled dome of Shah Nematollah Vali Shrine

Maybe there's a very big reason we like this kind of experience so much: we hope that life could be like this. Close-up, life feels complicated – a mixture of a million muddled things. We *want* our lives to be like this – rich and varied in all the different things that happen every day, but we *also* like structure, with a strong and clear overall pattern and meaning, like the predictable orbit of the Earth around the Sun.

We can find this sense of order in science: behind the millions of different things there are – birds and planets, snails and electricity, trees and copper – there are actually hidden rules that explain them all, and we can (through science) find out what they are.

This idea of beauty works for lots of things: a beautiful tree might have a simple overall shape but a complicated pattern of branches; a beautiful dress might be plain in outline, but it flows and flutters in a million different ways as you dance.

Beauty can be found in anything, from maths and nature to paintings and architecture, but it unfortunately isn't something people think about everyday. It can be interesting to investigate some things that *you* find very pleasing to look at.

Make a list of things you think are beautiful – maybe someone's face, a building, a vase or a flower (but it could be anything).

MY IDEAS OF BEAUTIFUL THINGS:

In what way is it complicated?
(Think of every single detail you see.)

In what way is it simple?
(Think of the overall pattern or outline.)

How is it complicated and simple at the same time?

This idea from Islamic art and science might not explain *everything* about beauty but it is quite a helpful idea.

Those artists and designers were interested in giving people a feeling of *harmony*: the experience you get when (even if only for a moment) you *feel* that all the funny little details add up to an ordered and calm and *beautiful* whole. Their goal in life wasn't getting more things or becoming famous or proving how wrong everyone else is – they wanted to create harmony. And maybe you do, too. So, perhaps when you think about what beauty means to you, you should be thinking a bit more about science.

Poland, 1542

Is There Something Wrong with Mars?

If you look up in the sky at various times on a sunny day, you see the Sun change position – moving always from east to west. From Earth, it might look like the Sun is moving and that our planet is staying still. Although we know now that's not the case, it's quite easy to see why hundreds of years ago people thought that the Earth was in a fixed position at the centre of everything. But scientists gradually realised that this couldn't be true.

But how did they discover this? What could possibly even suggest that we're orbiting the Sun? The answer involved looking closely at the night sky.

One of the nearest planets to us is Mars and you can see it on clear nights; it moves across the sky in a gentle and very slow arc, heading, night by night, gradually from the west to the east. Except *not* always. If you look very carefully, there are times when it seems to stand still and then go *backwards* before resuming its normal path.

Early scientists could see this happening, but they found it extremely tricky to explain. What could possibly be making this happen? Was Mars dancing about? Was it being pushed backwards by some unknown force? How could it possibly be behaving so strangely?

On The
Revolutions
Of The
Heavenl
Spheres
COPERNICUS

All the while, there was a much simpler answer just waiting to be given, yet for hundreds of years no one suggested it. The person who first presented the solution was a fascinating individual who lived mainly in Poland and was born towards the end of the 1400s, Nicolaus Copernicus.

Copernicus was interested in a lot of things, from maths to religion, art to astronomy. He didn't see being really interested in science as just a hobby. He thought science could tell us some very important things about the universe. Eventually, he realised that the movement of the Sun we see is because the Earth is spinning and orbiting the Sun.

Nicolaus Copernicus wrote about this in his book, called *On the Revolutions of the Heavenly Spheres*. It's a very clever title because revolution means going round (like the orbit of the Earth around the Sun), but it also quietly suggests something much bigger: we need a massive change (or revolution) in the way we think about some important things.

Copernicus showed that *we* here on Earth are moving; specifically, we are moving around the Sun – and later researchers discovered that Mars is, too. If you make this shift in *perspective*, you can see that Mars isn't going backwards at all. It's moving in its orbit the same way it always did; it's just that we're *overtaking* Mars in our orbit around the Sun.

Today, it's a little tricky to grasp the power of his idea, because we're always taught that the Sun is at the core of our Solar System and that we're the third planet in orbit, after Mercury and Venus and in front of Mars.

But the real power of what Copernicus was saying is different. The idea can also apply to how we see ourselves. We often grow up thinking that *we* are the centre of things. When you were younger, aged 4 or 6, you couldn't really imagine what a parent might do when they are not with you. You might not think that your teacher, for instance, might go dancing in the evening or go to the supermarket at the weekend to buy chocolate or have a beloved pet snake. We think people are what we see of them. We don't realise that they have their own orbits, just like we do. They're not just orbiting us.

Our version of Copernicus is to use observation and imagination to think about the lives of others, independent of ourselves.

What were Granny's ambitions when she was little?

Suppose your teacher wasn't a teacher, what else might they be doing?

What was your dad like when he was your age? What did he imagine his life as an adult might be like?

Imagine you are grown up and you have a child. What might you spend a lot of time thinking about apart from them?

Do you ever feel that people fuss too much about you?

These questions can feel pretty strange because they are asking us to do the Copernicus move: to think about the lives of others as not always revolving entirely around us.

But there's maybe a rather big upside to this as well. If you're not the centre of the universe, it means that not everyone is looking at you or thinking about you all the time. You can do the things you want without worrying so much about what other people think. Everyone is involved in their own orbit more than you might suppose.

A lot of people felt annoyed with Copernicus because they thought he was saying the Earth wasn't important because it wasn't the middle of everything. But maybe what they missed was how nice it might be to not be at the centre of things all the time.

China, 1500s

The Discovery of Inoculation

One of the most basic things we want is to keep ourselves and those we love safe. We want to protect ourselves and others. That's a lovely idea. But how, really, can we do it?

A first, and very natural, idea is to keep everything bad away. We want to make sure that nothing upsetting or difficult comes their (or our) way. But this may not be the most sensible plan. Science has a slightly different, surprising – and maybe rather helpful – story to tell. Let's start by looking at something horrible.

Long ago, as early as 1350 BCE, practically all round the world, there was a terrible disease called smallpox. It was a virus that caused flu-like symptoms such as headaches and a fever, and also led to a painful rash that formed spots filled with pus. It spread rapidly and killed around 30 per cent of people who caught it. Obviously, you'd want to protect people from getting smallpox. But what would be the best way of doing that? You could try to *avoid* it, by living far away from other people and being totally self-sufficient.

But for most people that wasn't an option. If you lived in a town or a village, it would be very hard to avoid people. You would still need to get food and go to work, and get water from the local well, which would have been shared by lots of people.

But there was one crucial ray of hope: quite a lot of people who caught the virus didn't die. They'd get very sick for a while, but they survived. And once they were better, they very rarely got smallpox again. Why not? Why did getting the illness *once* – and surviving – give you some kind of protection in the future?

All sorts of suggestions must have been floating around. Maybe the illness was a kind of test from the gods, and if you passed the test, you wouldn't need to be tested again. Maybe smallpox was like a magical curse that could only be used once on anyone.

Starting in Africa and Asia, some clever people – who were like scientists (but remember the word science hadn't been invented yet!) – developed a very different idea. Maybe surviving meant your body had *learned* how to fight and defeat the illness; so, once your body knew how to fight off smallpox, you'd be much safer from it in the future.

You could imagine the disease like an invading army. It's ferocious, but if you dig big holes in the ground, the enemy will fall straight into them and won't be able to get any further. When you catch the disease, your body's immune system responds and tries to defend your body against infection – the equivalent of digging traps. Once the holes are there, if the enemy attacks again in the future, they will just fall into the holes again. And this kind of thinking about what the body was doing gave rise to a scary but brilliant idea. The best thing – in terms of staying safe – would be to get a very mild dose of smallpox. It wouldn't be enough to really harm you, and your body would learn the trick of digging holes and trapping the invaders: responding to the virus and fighting it off. Then, if it came back, you'd be well-prepared.

From the mid-1500s, Chinese doctors started doing something that was very insightful. They would deliberately give people the smallest possible amounts of the disease by gathering dried smallpox scabs, grinding them up and then blowing them into the nostril of the patient using a pipe. They'd almost all survive and then be safe for a long time after that.

The idea was called *inoculation* or *variolation*. It later got another more familiar name: *vaccination*.

The first proper smallpox vaccine was developed in England in the late 1700s. Edward Jenner, a country doctor, noticed that milkmaids who had contracted a much milder cattle disease called cowpox were unlikely to contract smallpox. Jenner experimented with taking pus from a cowpox scab and scratching it into the skin of an 8-year-old boy. The boy felt mildly ill with the cowpox virus and then recovered. When the boy was later introduced to smallpox, he did not develop the disease.

From this research, Jenner developed his vaccine, giving children a minute dose of cowpox – so little that they wouldn't get sick but just enough to teach their bodies how to get rid of it. That meant that when they actually encountered smallpox, they were fine. He persuaded governments around the world to do this, so today no one suffers from the disease.

Deliberately infecting people might sound scary, but it worked. It worked so well that it was gradually adopted around the world. In the past, millions of people died from smallpox. But thanks to vaccinations, since 1978 no one has.

But the idea of inoculation does not just apply to our physical health. It suggests that there are other situations in which we might need to develop our resistance and resilience.

For instance, it's not very nice when someone disagrees with you or says they don't like your ideas. And so, you might imagine the best thing would be if this never happened. You might try to isolate yourself and keep your opinions to yourself because you're worried they will disagree with you.

But the better strategy is a kind of inoculation: teaching your brain the right kinds of tricks for dealing with the problem. What might some of these inoculating tricks be? Instead of getting angry with the person, you could ask them: *why do you think that?* Go slowly, remain calm and listen to what the other person is saying. Listening isn't the same as agreeing, but it can help you see things from their point of view.

There might be more than one good idea here. Perhaps you're both sort of right. Even if you think you are right, you don't have to convince them. You can be fine without their agreement. Maybe you end up being wrong and they turn out to be right, but that's OK because everybody is wrong sometimes. It's OK to change your mind: that's what learning is often about.

So, here are some questions that you could ask yourself and think about how you might answer:

Do you ever get into disagreements with people? What about?

Is it sometimes an upsetting experience? Do you get impatient, annoyed or angry? Do you feel like they are attacking you?

Are there inoculating ideas you could try (from the list above, maybe) that might make you better able to cope with disagreement?

Could you try one or two of them out for real?

You are not trying to get rid of disagreement – because all interesting projects in life involve encountering disagreement. What you are trying to do is get more resilient and better at coping with it.

England, 1660s

The Secrets of Light

One of the central factors that affect human life – and indeed the lives of many creatures and even plants – is the difference between night and day. The presence or absence of sunlight shapes the way we live.

But what actually *is* light? What is it made of and how does it work? People must have been asking themselves such questions for thousands of years.

But no one made much progress in understanding what was really going on until an epidemic, often referred to as the 'Great Plague', broke out in London in 1665 and started to spread throughout England. Anyone who could left the cities, and a lot of students were sent home from school and university, including a young student called Isaac Newton, who was studying at the University of Cambridge. He had to go back to live with his mother on a rather nice family farm in the countryside. He didn't get on at all well with his mother and once – when he was in a *very* bad mood – he thought about burning the farmhouse down. That's a terrible idea, of course, and he didn't actually do it, but it's interesting: Isaac Newton was about as clever as a human being can possibly be, in terms of being great at maths and science, but he struggled when it came to emotions.

While he was stuck at home, he decided to turn one of the old barns into a sort of laboratory and study the things that interested him – maths, physics and light.

He made the room completely dark, except for a tiny hole he made in one of the window covers that let in a narrow ray of daylight. Then he placed a thick wedge of glass (called a prism) on a table so that the beam of light went right into it.

When he got the positioning of the prism just right, something lovely happened: the light seemed to spread out and made a sort of straight rainbow on the far wall. All the different colours were there and always in the same order: red, orange, yellow, green, blue, indigo (which is a sort of dark blue) and violet (which is a bit like purple).

People had tried this before. But what Newton did next was new. Newton inserted a second prism into the spreading rays of light and – to his complete surprise – all the different colours joined back together to make ordinary white light.

What could possibly be going on? What Newton was discovering in his old barn was that daylight (the light that comes from the Sun) is actually made up of a huge number of slightly different sorts of light – and each one looks a slightly different colour to our eyes when we see them separately. Today, we think of light as being made up of waves of different lengths, and these different wavelengths produce different colours.

Newton realised that it is light that determines the colour of objects. A leaf looks green to us because its surface reflects only certain wavelengths of light. The leaf absorbs all the colours of light that hit it, except for green light, which it reflects back to us. It is an incredibly small difference in wavelength that makes things appear different colours to us.

This wasn't anything like the end of the story of light. Other scientists took Newton's ideas further and discovered even more about light, including that there are many colours our eyes can't see, and our brains can't even imagine. We see only a very small part of the rays that actually make up sunlight, and if our eyes and brains were different, we'd be able to see thousands of new colours. It's a thought to make your head spin.

Much later, scientists discovered that light is travelling incredibly quickly. Not just fast, but insanely fast: at 300,000 km *per second*, which is around 24 million times faster than the fastest human has ever run.

We tend to think that science – and basically being clever – is all about understanding important or unusual things. You might think someone is clever because they know what 'euphony' means (it means a pleasant sound, particularly the sound of words) or because they know that in Ancient Greek myths, Cerberus was a dog with three heads.

But Newton was pointing in a very different direction. He was interested in something extremely ordinary and everyday: sunlight. And by studying it carefully, he worked something out that had been puzzling people for centuries.

You might discover that some of the biggest questions about life can be answered by looking at ordinary, everyday things: what really is happiness or sadness all about? How do people end up in jobs they like?

It means, too, that the exciting things might really be obvious. It can sound as if it's more exciting to trek through the Andes mountains than to go to the supermarket, or that it must be more fun to go snowboarding than to have a flute lesson. But Newton – and his science experiments at the family farm – suggest something different. Locked inside ordinary things, there's a world of colour and fascination and mystery. If you think deeply about some important questions like Newton did, you might finally start asking the right questions that help you discover the answer to something that's been bugging you for ages.

Think about your normal route to school. What are the nicer things you notice along the way? Why do you like them?

When people disagree, is it because they don't properly listen to – or properly understand – what each other is saying?

What is boredom? Why do some people get bored more quickly than others? What makes you feel bored? Why those things?

Why do people get upset (including you)? Where does anger and irritation come from?

Imagine you are the Isaac Newton of going to school, or of disagreement or of feeling fed up (three super-common things). What would it be like if millions and billions of people really thought very hard about these things?

The Netherlands, 1670s

The Horror and Delight of Microscopes

Human beings have known about glass for a very long time, though until about 150 years ago it was rare and expensive. (In old houses, the panes of glass are usually quite small because people simply didn't know how to make big, thin sheets of glass.) A wonderful thing about glass is that it's solid – it keeps out the rain and the wind – but you can also see through it.

But there's an even more special thing about glass: depending on its shape, it can *distort* how things look. If you look at a pencil through an empty water glass, the pencil looks like it's bending all over the place and sometimes it looks even thinner, as it would if it were farther away, or thicker, as if it were closer to you.

These strange effects depend on the exact shape of the glass, and if you try a lot of experiments, you will find that a certain shape of glass always makes things look bigger.

Around the late 16th century, a Dutch spectacle maker named Zacharias Janssen experimented with special pieces of glass – called lenses – and invented a new instrument for making small things look bigger: the microscope. Early versions of the microscope could magnify objects by up to 30 times their size.

A few decades later, a Dutch civil servant and scientist, Antonie van Leeuwenhoek, made an even more powerful microscope. He made a lens that could magnify things to more than two hundred times their size. That's really tiny. Leeuwenhoek used his microscope to study blood cells, minerals, plant tissue – lots of things that we'd never been able to see in such detail before. And while he was looking, he discovered tiny organisms called bacteria, which opened up a whole new world of study for scientists, known as microbiology.

If you look at a droplet of seawater magnified three hundred times, you might get a bit of a fright. When you look at it with the naked eye, it looks completely pure and perfect. But it actually contains all sorts of very tiny things swimming around in it. These are called microorganisms, or microbes. You might think, *Oh no, I must be looking at a drop of poisonous, disgusting filthy water*. But no, this is just what completely normal seawater looks like when seen in great detail.

It's a pretty weird discovery. And at first, maybe it makes you never want to swim in the sea again. But it has a lot to teach us. Microscopes are all about looking closely and finding out things that you couldn't see before.

Things that are actually totally fine can *look* a bit ghastly if you see them very close up. And the place where this actually matters most has nothing to do with water and everything to do with people.

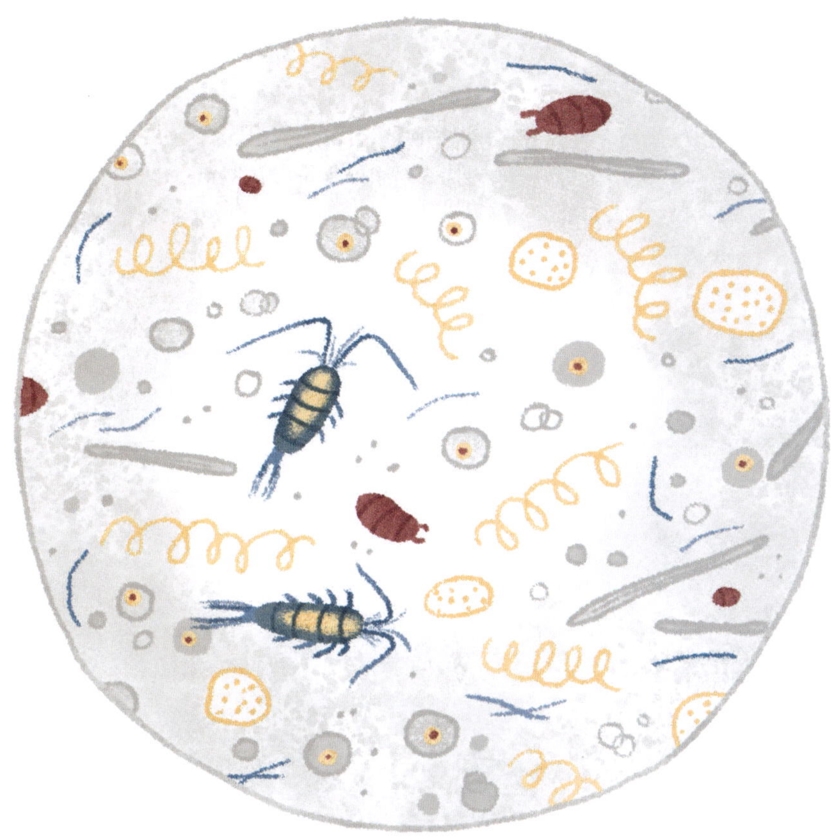

Imagine you kind of know someone who seems really nice. You want to get to know them better. But, when you try and talk to them, they turn out to be a bit rude or ignore you. What has happened? Have you been deceived? A good way of thinking about this is that getting to know someone really well is like putting a drop of water under the microscope. We need to examine things more closely. The person might seem rude now, but when you get to see the tiny details, they may not be like they appear on the surface; there will always be the equivalent of little microbes, or details, still to be discovered. It might not be that they are being rude on purpose. When you look closer you might notice that they're sad or worried or afraid.

When you get to know them better, and look more closely, you discover more about who they are. Not everything might be good; they will be short tempered on some occasions, or silly, or ask too many questions, or not enough about yourself. But the same is true of you.

But there was something else that the new microscopes also revealed: unexpected beauty. A snowflake, as it falls from the sky, is just a minute white fleck – of no interest in itself; we usually only care about what billions and trillions of snowflakes do together: turn the streets and fields white and magical.

But under the microscope, each snowflake has an astonishing, delicate and unique pattern. It's actually made up of little symmetrical branches, each one then branching out farther in turn. It's like a tiny work of art. It was a deeply puzzling and exciting discovery. Why on Earth do such tiny things have such wonderfully beautiful shapes? How does it happen? How do they get to be like that? The individual beauty of snowflakes had always been hidden from human awareness – until someone thought of shaping glass very cleverly to make lenses and focusing their attention on the tiny details. When you become friends with someone, you start to see all the details about them that make them beautiful and unique.

What do you notice that other people you know tend to overlook?

What important things about you do other people tend to overlook?

Science encourages us to look at all the details before deciding how we really feel about someone or something. But this can feel a bit odd, only because we don't usually think about other people in this way. Put any drop of water – or any person – under the microscope and they (and we) all turn out to be pretty interesting, beautiful and also, in some ways, off-putting.

Except that's normal. It's not a strange revelation about you or other people. The closer you look, the more accurate picture you can build of what people (including you) are like.

The Galápagos Islands, 1830s

Evolution and Self-compassion

Imagine you are living a very long time ago – hundreds and hundreds of years ago – and you wonder: *how did everything come to be the way it is?* Why are there tigers and butterflies, whales and buttercups? Where did they all come from?

There was really no available answer other than that *someone* – some super powerful and brilliant creator – had designed them all from scratch. This was called *the argument from design*: it said, in effect, the natural world is so beautiful, organised and elegant it must be the result of some great creative genius that designed it all; there must have been a cosmic artist who tinted the rose, gave the giraffe its splendid neck or the turtle its amazing hard shell. Divine intervention was the only explanation anyone could come up with. It was actually unreasonable *not* to believe. Although it certainly didn't mean that everyone agreed on who this godly creator might be.

It wasn't until the early 19th century that these ideas started to change, and it was largely thanks to a very unlikely person: a quiet, sensitive young man called Charles Darwin. Born in England, Darwin was rather hopeless at school and university (he found most subjects boring, especially Latin); but he was also – fortunately for us and for science – fascinated by the natural world, and from a kindly, well-to-do family, which allowed him to pursue his interests.

In his early 20s, Darwin was offered an unusual opportunity. A slight acquaintance was captaining a ship on a voyage, pretty much around the world, to map various bits of coastline that were still uncertain. The captain asked Darwin to come along as his companion. Darwin agreed and set off on a five-year science expedition to South America where he took on the role of the ship's naturalist (a person who studies living things).

During the expedition, Darwin spent a lot of time taking notes about all the different kinds of animals and plants he saw as they travelled about. It took him nearly twenty years to work out what it all meant, but eventually, when he was about 50, he wrote a book called *On the Origin of Species.*

Darwin's big idea was that animals and plants gradually change and develop (evolve) over long periods of time to survive and flourish in different places.

Suppose you are a very early kind of giraffe, living in a place where there are tall trees and you really like eating leaves – but there are lots of other creatures that like them, too. Any giraffe with a slightly longer neck gets an advantage: it can reach the higher leaves that the others miss and so can find more to eat. The longer-necked ones survive, and they have offspring that share this feature (just as, with humans, really tall parents are more likely to have tall children). Now the longest-necked ones of the next generation have even more of an advantage, and they do well and pass on their super long necks to *their* offspring.

Giraffes weren't designed by anyone; they gradually evolved to have longer necks through a natural process called selection. Longer necks simply helped giraffes survive, and so necks got longer and longer over thousands of years.

That makes sense about giraffes. But what does it mean for humans? Darwin's theory of natural selection suggested that human beings must have evolved too, sharing a common ancestor with early kinds of apes.

Over hundreds of thousands of years, early humans evolved from solitary, nomadic types to living in large groups – finding berries and teaming up to go hunting.

But then what happened? Quite recently, we've massively changed how we live. In just a few generations – which is much too short for evolution – we have started to live in cities, are much less active as we spend a lot of time sitting at desks at school or work; we live in small families and money is now an important part of how we live. We live a kind of life that is very different to the one we evolved for. And that creates unexpected problems.

For instance, humans tend to like sweet things. That made evolutionary sense. For hundreds and thousands of generations, the only sweet things that were easy to find were pieces of fruit. So, our sweet tooth directed us to eat healthy things. Those who guzzled more apples or more wild strawberries were more likely to survive.

But today, this once hugely helpful instinct has become a bit of a problem. Now we can very cheaply make all the sugar we can possibly eat; so our love of sweet things directs us towards chocolate or ice cream instead of fruit or vegetables – not the healthiest choices.

The same has happened around our attention span. A great thing about humans, as we evolved, was that no matter what else we were doing, we would instantly be drawn to the sight of small, coloured, moving things. We had to be; it might be a snake! Our brains are hyper-responsive to new or unusual movement.

But today, this can cause us difficulties. You are supposed to be paying attention to a maths lesson, but there's a fly climbing up the window that keeps distracting you, and your brain automatically gives up on long division. You should sleep at night, but it is more enticing to keep on watching music videos.

Darwin, unexpectedly, is explaining why modern life can sometimes be a bit difficult. The things we evolved to do no longer particularly help us. And that's not entirely our fault. We didn't evolve to sit at desks for hours every day or take exams. So, if we're having a hard time concentrating at school, we actually deserve a lot of compassion for ourselves.

What do you find difficult to control in your own behaviour?

How might that be connected to evolution?

What sort of help might actually help?

Darwin – and science – is saying it's understandable that you find lots of things difficult because in the modern world we sometimes have to do things that go against our own nature. Maybe we have to, but we deserve a bit of sympathy as we try (and often fail) to do what others expect of us.

USA, 1860s

How to Date a Dinosaur

Long before anyone arrived from Europe, the Oglala Lakota people, native to what we now call South Dakota in the USA, would often come across large, fossilised bones. They didn't resemble the bones of any animal they knew, and they came to think of them as the remains of monsters. Similar discoveries had been made from time to time in other places, too: in China, people thought they might be the bones of dragons; in Ancient Greece, they were said to be the skeletons of giants.

It was only in the middle of the 19th century, however, that bones such as these were carefully collected and put together – and the shapes of the astonishing (and sometimes terrifying) creatures started to emerge. It must have been quite extraordinary to have been amongst the first visitors to the Academy of Natural Sciences in Philadelphia to see – in 1868 – the more than 25-feet long skeleton of what we today know to be a dinosaur.

Slowly, scientists started to get more accurate ideas of what these creatures looked like, but one huge question remained to be answered: *when* did they actually live?

It was a surprisingly hard question to answer. Human records that describe when events happened only go back a few thousand years. What happened before that? How much happened before that? Was there a long period of life on Earth before there were humans? Nobody knew for certain because no one had been around to write things down.

There's actually no obvious evidence at all. You look at a mountain and ask, how long has it been there? Ten thousand years, a million years, a hundred million, much more? These are vast differences, but nothing you can see gives you the slightest clue. It took a great deal of scientific investigation – which had nothing to do with dinosaurs or mountains directly – to find the answer. And it turned out to be to do with atoms (the tiny particles that make up everything in the universe – you will find out more about these on pages 102–107). It was thanks to all the complicated work scientists in laboratories were doing to understand atoms that – eventually – it was possible to date the dinosaurs.

The great idea involved a metal called potassium. A special kind of potassium is found in the lava that spews from volcanoes. This special potassium isn't entirely stable. Through a complex process called decay, it produces a gas called argon, which gets trapped inside the lava.

When a volcano erupts, the lava is boiling hot, causing any argon in the lava to escape. As the lava cools down, it solidifies and turns into rock. The newly solidifying lava doesn't contain any argon gas inside it at all. But as the years and centuries pass, the level of argon trapped inside the rock starts to build up. This is an incredibly slow process: it takes billions of years for all the potassium to transform into argon.

But that's brilliant, because if you measure very carefully, you can tell how much of this gas has been produced: the more gas present in the lava, the longer the time since the volcano erupted. Fortunately (for us), dinosaur bones were often found among layers of volcanic deposits, making it possible to calculate how long ago the fossils had been buried – and therefore when the dinosaur must have lived. The answers were completely staggering. The rocks in which the bones were found were maybe 100, 150 or even 200 million years old. It suddenly became clear that dinosaurs didn't just live a long time ago, they lived an incredibly long time ago.

Even with all the scientific evidence, we can struggle to understand the reality of the past. We know, of course, that many events happened a long time ago, but we can't quite grasp what this really means or how it relates to us now. For example, when you are little, it's hard to believe that your parents were ever *really* children; or that your grandparents had grandparents, who had their own grandparents ... You gradually realise an amazing thing: that the past was very, very long and that you are only living in a tiny part of a long history.

Try to find a picture of a parent or grandparent when they were little. Their hairstyles and clothes probably look pretty strange. But try to imagine that for them – in that moment – that *was* the present. They were the new generation, the cutting edge. They couldn't wait for (or dreaded) what 1973 or 2003 would bring.

Then imagine someone in fifty or sixty years' time looking at a photo of *you* from this very moment.

How might they feel about you?

Will they think you look funny?

Do you think they will understand what it meant for you to live today?

For them, your *now* is in the long-ago past, but for you, *now* is totally real.

It's a very strange exercise that can make your head spin. But maybe it's worth it. Quite often, it's tempting to treat the past as if it was just a lot of old bones buried in rock. But it wasn't like that.

It was completely real: it was 'today'. And one day, we will be seen as the equivalent of dinosaurs by a future we cannot yet imagine.

Vienna, 19th century

Why We Get Angry with Ourselves

At the very end of the 19th century, a youngish medical student called Sigmund Freud was doing a lot of experiments on eels. He wasn't especially interested in fish, rather he was trying to get some more general ideas – that might also apply to humans – about how the nervous system, which includes the brain, actually functions.

Freud soon moved on from fish, and when he qualified as a doctor, he started to form interesting theories about how our minds work. In order to investigate this further, he started asking his patients what they really felt about themselves. He wanted to understand what was actually going on in the minds of others (and no doubt, secretly, he wanted to make sense of what was going on in *his* mind, too). This scientific study of the mind and the ways that people think and behave is called *psychology*.

One thing he discovered was both shocking and yet extremely familiar. He discovered that lots of people are immensely – and often unfairly – self-critical. A rather nice, good natured, well-intentioned person would turn up at his office, and by asking very careful questions, Freud would discover that this person saw themselves as foolish, a monster, a failure, a fake. No one meeting them on the street or at a party would ever guess the incredibly mean things they were saying to themselves in the privacy of their own heads.

It seemed very unfair. These people usually tried very hard indeed to be kind to others, and they might, in fact, do lots of things rather well. Yet, they still felt, deep within their private thoughts, that they were not good enough. And it wasn't just one or two people who felt like this. If you were to encourage any rather nice person to open up in the right way, they would likely admit to thinking the same kinds of harsh thoughts about themselves sometimes. The big question was:

Why would this be happening? Why do people who are actually entirely lovely so often end up thinking badly of themselves?

Freud's rather brilliant idea was that as we grow, we don't just learn facts; we absorb a picture of what we are meant to be like that is impossibly perfect. No one does – or could – live up to this standard, and yet we think we should.

We are like animals – like cats and crocodiles – who have millions of natural instincts: to snap or hiss at someone who annoys us, to laze in the sun, to run away and hide, to keep whatever we want just for ourselves. We have all these impulses bubbling up, but also, we have this ideal image of what we're supposed to be like. Sometimes it can feel like we are caught in the middle: we do our best but sometimes we fail.

Suppose Mum says you can't do something you want to. The instinctual animal part of you wants to scream and shout. But the 'ideal' part of you wants to be good. If you say, 'You're ruining everything!', you feel terrible: you've said something horrible to Mum, and you don't really mean it. But if you say, 'Yes, of course', you still wish you didn't have to, and maybe it feels like you're only pretending to be obedient. Whatever you do, it feels wrong.

This is a moment to ask some interesting questions ...

When do you feel annoyed with yourself?

What words or ideas come into your head when you feel you've failed or been bad?

Imagine a nice friend told you these sorts of things about themselves? What might you say to them? How might you be kind to them?

When we judge ourselves too harshly, at root it is actually an exaggerated version of something really impressive and wonderful about the human brain: we can realise we might be wrong.

It's beautiful and important to realise that we're not perfect – no one is. By understanding this, we can have an idea of what we might do better; we can feel sorry for our mistakes. We can realise that it's OK to make mistakes or be wrong about something, and when we are, we should treat ourselves as kindly as we would treat a friend.

Freud, essentially, was showing the idea of 'being perfect' could lead us to feel miserable. As he saw it, the issue is not to stop trying to be better or making demands on yourself, but to have more realistic, wiser expectations. A curious and important idea is that being less critical of yourself is actually linked to understanding yourself and other people *better.* It feels as if your harsh thoughts are brilliant insights, but maybe they are often very inaccurate.

Freud is raising one of the biggest questions: how can we be sympathetic (to ourselves and to others) about our failures and mistakes? How can we actually help another person (or ourselves) be better? Saying 'You are terrible' doesn't actually do anything to bring about a better result. In fact, it works in the opposite direction; it undermines anyone's feeling that they can improve.

Freud brought us to the cusp of one of the great positive questions of all time: *how do we actually help ourselves and others to overcome our (or their) problems?* Pointing out the problem is almost never the relevant factor. The tricky (but brilliant) thing is to describe the easily workable steps by which improvement would be made. Think of what the best possible teacher is like. They don't make you feel bad about not knowing, they make you feel confident you can learn. With this in mind, we can all learn to be kinder to ourselves.

CRITICAL THOUGHT:

I always mess up.

MORE ACCURATE ASSERTION:

I occasionally mess up (like everyone does) but mostly I'm quite good at lots of things.

CRITICAL THOUGHT:

I must be good otherwise my parent will be upset.

MORE ACCURATE ASSERTION:

My parent will love me, even if I disagree with them.

CRITICAL THOUGHT:

X doesn't like me because I'm a failure.

MORE ACCURATE ASSERTION:

X doesn't think that at all. I just think they do.

CRITICAL THOUGHT:

Everyone else finds this easy. I'm the only one having trouble.

MORE ACCURATE ASSERTION:

Nearly everyone finds this subject difficult, only they don't tell me (just as I don't tell them).

UK, 1910s

The Big Truth about Atoms

The idea of an 'atom' was imagined long, long ago in ancient Greece. The philosopher Democritus thought that everything must be made up of tiny particles, which he believed were solid, indestructible and indivisible. At the time, nobody knew, but logically the answer seemed to be that there surely must be some kind of basic, and extremely tiny, building blocks out of which things are made.

To understand the idea of atoms, we can conduct a fascinating thought experiment. Suppose you cut something in half – a bar of gold, say, to make it glamorous. You end up with two smaller pieces, of course! What's interesting about that? Well, suppose you cut one of the halves in half again. And then cut that piece in half. Before long, you are dealing with something so small you can hardly see it.

But suppose you had super powerful eyes and an amazingly sharp knife (though please don't think about trying this; it's a thought experiment, not something to try at home. Anyway, we're guessing you don't have a gold bar on hand to try this out). As you keep on halving and halving, you wonder if you could keep on going forever, or would you finally arrive at something that you couldn't cut, no matter how incredibly sharp the knife you had?

It wasn't until the early 19th century that scientists began to discover what atoms might really be. They are the tiny particles that everything is made up of. Most of the materials we encounter day to day can be broken down in laboratories. For example, a water molecule is made up of oxygen and hydrogen atoms. Through a special chemical reaction, you can split the water molecule to produce two gases: oxygen and hydrogen. But whatever scientists did, they couldn't get those gases to break down any further. You could combine them with many other substances, but you couldn't split them into simpler components. The same was true of gold, silver and copper, and a handful of other 'elements', as they became known.

And so, it must have seemed like the end of a huge journey of investigation. After many centuries of trying to find out, careful experiments had revealed the few basic building blocks out of which everything else was made. If you had these 'elemental' things, you could – in principle – combine them into absolutely anything. But there were still some questions.

Why were atoms different from one another?

Why did an oxygen atom behave so differently to a gold atom? (For example, pure oxygen is a gas, while pure gold is solid and quite heavy.)

And gradually, the slightly unsettling idea started to take hold: atoms must contain things inside them that make them different. An atom isn't – can't be – the most basic unit. It must have even tinier components inside it that make it the way it is.

So, what could these things possibly be? In 1911, a physicist called Ernest Rutherford – originally from New Zealand but working at the University of Manchester in the UK – discovered the very surprising answer. He found that most of an atom is empty space, with a tiny nucleus at its centre. This inspired another physicist called Niels Bohr to work out that even tinier particles called electrons orbit this nucleus (as their name suggests, electrons have a lot to do with electricity). And a bit later on, scientists discovered that the nucleus contains tiny subatomic particles called protons and neutrons.

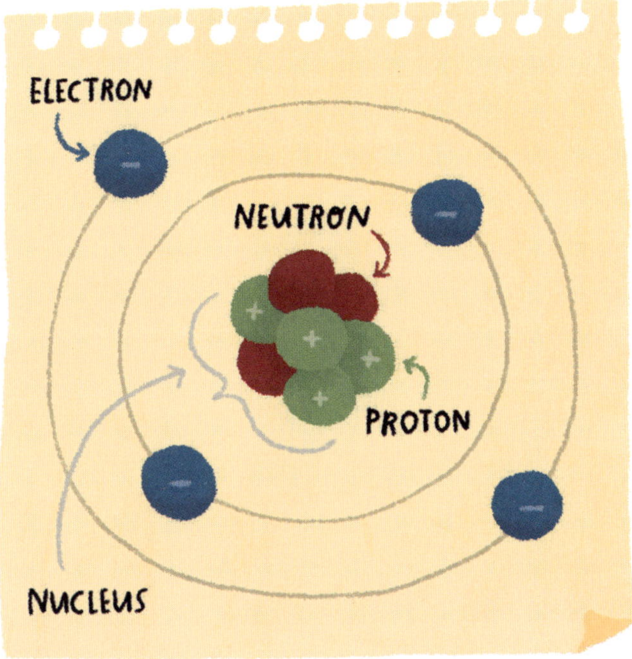

Again, it must have seemed as if the final answer had been reached. But people started to ask: what are protons and neutrons made of? The terrifying, exciting thing was that the more scientists found out about what really goes on inside atoms, the stranger the answers started to get. Electrons behave in incredibly bizarre ways; and it turns out that protons and neutrons are made up of even smaller particles called quarks.

If you look at the story as a whole, there's a very interesting pattern. At each key moment, there must have been a feeling of, 'Oh, now we have got it! At last, we finally understand. Yes, there are atoms! That's it'. But then new and harder questions arose: what are atoms made of? And the scientists answered that: protons, neutrons and electrons. Brilliant! But what are they made of? Instead of getting simpler, the answers became more and more complex and strange. This wasn't because scientists were making mistakes. Things got stranger *because* they were gaining a deeper understanding.

It can be a bit like this in life. When you're 3, you might think: *when I'm 5, I'll basically understand everything*. And then when you're 5 you think, *when I'm 10, I will*. But by the time you actually are 10, you realise there's even more you don't understand than you ever expected.

Our brains like to tell us that the more we know, the clearer everything will become. However, the story of science – especially around atoms – suggests the opposite: the more you understand, the more questions arise, and the more complicated and strange things become.

And sorry to disappoint you, but you won't have all the answers when you're grown up either, and that's OK. Maybe you could find out what clever grown-ups are confused about. Not minor (though annoying) things like when your next swimming lesson is or where the next winter Olympics will be held, but the really big and important things: what is love? What makes people unhappy? What makes a really good government? What is beauty? Why are some people nicer than others?

It's OK to feel puzzled and confused. It doesn't mean you are ignorant or unintelligent. In fact, it's the opposite reason: things are just genuinely very hard to understand and make sense of. You are clever enough to grasp how strange and confusing human existence really is.

Austria, c.1890s

The Mystery of Heat

What could be more obvious: some things are hot, and some things are cold. If you put a cold thing (like cold water) in a hot thing (like a hot bath), the hot thing cools down, so you can get in without burning your toes.

But why does this happen? How does the cold get into the hot water? How does heat work, really?

It took an incredibly long time to answer this simple sounding question, and that's because we can't *see* what's really happening. People needed to understand other things *before* they could comprehend heat – and even then, the answer was hard to believe.

A first big clue comes from a simple observation that can be shown in an experiment. Suppose you put an ice cube on a plate in the sun. At first, the cube is hard, but as the sun warms it, it starts to melt, leaving a little puddle.

What's happening? Ice is made of water, of course, which means it's made of H_2O molecules – two atoms of hydrogen and one atom of oxygen that cling to each other. These molecules each have a tiny little bit of attraction called hydrogen bonding, which means they are attracted to each other and get pulled together.

An ice cube is solid because the water molecules are pulled together tightly. So tightly that the pressure of your finger, for instance, isn't enough to separate them. That's what 'solid' means: the molecules that make up the substance are pulled together so tightly that they stick together even when you press on them. The molecules in ice are held in fixed positions and cannot really move about.

When the ice starts to warm up, it melts and becomes a liquid. It becomes runny – if you touch the water, it moves. The molecules are still attracting each other, but not nearly as strongly as when they are in a solid state. The molecules in water are not held in fixed positions and can move about. So, the pressure from your finger is enough to move them out of the way, which is why you can dive into a swimming pool. However, water can also support you because, although the molecules move, it takes some force to move them a lot (try walking through waist-deep water).

When water molecules are heated more, they become a gas (steam). They move so fast they pull apart from each other, so it takes almost no effort at all to push them apart. You could run easily through a cloud of steam (though it would be incredibly hot!), but also you can't swim in steam: it won't support you.

But this led to a strange realisation: heat is just how fast the molecules are moving – the faster they move, the more heat energy they have.

So, amazingly, people couldn't make sense of heat until they understood molecules and how atoms work.

When something is heated, its particles move faster. They bump into other particles more often, transferring some of their energy and making those particles move faster, too. This is why heat moves from hotter to cooler things: the energy is being shared between them. The fast molecules slightly slow down, the slow ones slightly speed up and the temperature evens out – allowing you to put your toe in the bath.

These discoveries were made by Ludwig Boltzmann, a scientist living in Austria, who worked all this out in the 1890s. But at the time no one believed him, which made him very unhappy.

What we're exploring is how surprisingly long it can take to understand something, even if the question feels basic. Why does an ice cube melt in the sunshine? To answer this (as we have been seeing), you need to understand quite a lot of behind-the-scenes stuff. You have to know about atoms and molecules and how they attract each other and move. These are complex ideas, which can be really hard for people to fully understand.

Quite a lot of problems are actually rather like this. You feel you *should* be able to answer them because they sound simple.

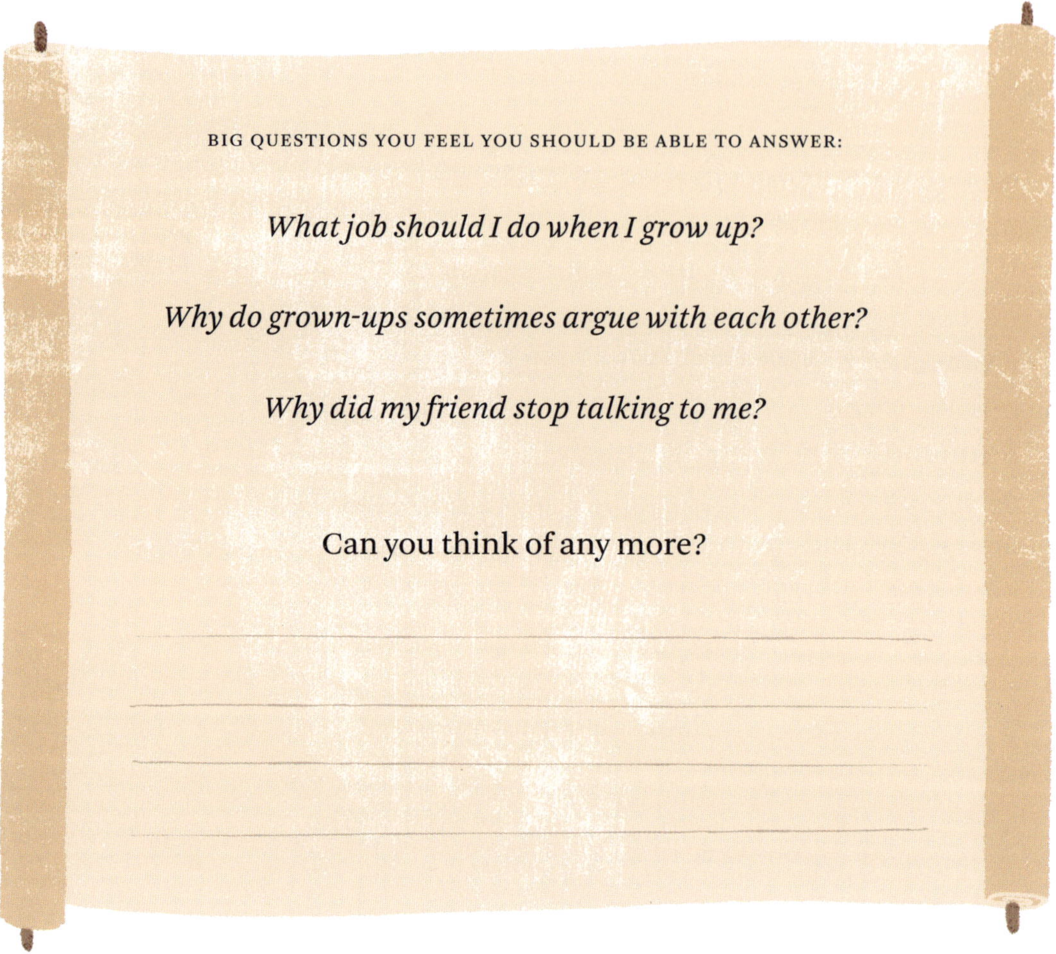

They may *sound* easy – and are *very* important to ask – but finding the answers is sometimes more difficult because you need to understand what might be going on around things you can't directly see.

That doesn't mean there aren't clear answers; only that the answers might not be so obvious, or what you expected. And it might – very reasonably – take quite a long time to understand the answers. It's natural to confuse not being able to find an answer *yet* with the feeling that you'll *never* find a good and reasonable answer.

At what age do you think you should understand:

What it means to be a good friend

Why quite a lot of relationships don't work out

Why the world is quite bad at dealing with collective problems

We are unfair to ourselves when we suppose we should be able to answer such questions immediately. We might feel that the answer must be obvious and that we're missing something because we can't work it out.

What we're saying is that a question can be important and natural to ask, and, at the same time, very complicated to answer. It might be totally understandable – in fact, unavoidable – that it may take ages to find the answer. We should not get too frustrated if we can't come up with an answer today.

20th century

The Secret Needs of Plants

Plants need water and sunlight to grow. People have known this for as long as there has been agriculture, which started many thousands of years ago. Then, in the 18th century, a new and pretty surprising and puzzling fact was discovered.

Plants also need carbon dioxide (CO_2) gas to grow. This is unexpected because normally we think of this gas as 'bad' and a problem. When we breathe out, we release carbon dioxide. A room with a little too much carbon dioxide feels stuffy and unpleasant to us, and its build-up in the atmosphere is an important factor in global warming. But plants can't live without it. Why?

At the time, nobody could properly explain this. It was only in the 20th century, when enough was known about how atoms work, that scientists could understand what was happening to the carbon dioxide molecules and why.

Carbon dioxide, as the name suggests, is a molecule made up of carbon (the same element found in coal and diamonds) and oxygen. The plant also takes in water from the soil. Water is a molecule made up of hydrogen and oxygen. Using the energy of the Sun, a plant starts the process of photosynthesis.

During photosynthesis, the plant uses the carbon dioxide to make glucose (a type of sugar) and transforms the water into oxygen. It uses the carbon to produce glucose, while releasing the oxygen. The hydrogen from the water is also used in making the glucose.

So, why does the plant need to do this? Well, glucose is the primary source of energy for plants, and they need it to grow and develop. But the plant doesn't need all the oxygen it produces, so it releases what it doesn't need back into the air – which is lovely for us because oxygen is what *we* need to breathe.

This creates a really unique relationship between us and plants: they need the carbon dioxide we breathe out and don't really want in the atmosphere; they use it to grow and make stuff we love to eat. Then as a kind of leftovers (from their point of view) they release oxygen, which is essential for our survival. It means that plants play a much more fundamental role in the world than people had previously imagined – not just as a source of food and beauty, but also in regulating the atmosphere.

But what could the life of a plant, or the discovery of photosynthesis, tell you about yourself and your own life?

The first question is:

What do you need in order to flourish, in order to grow and do and make the best things you can?

When it comes to plants, water and sunshine were always obvious, but no one for a long time understood about the need for carbon dioxide. What might your version of that be? What might you need that's not obvious?

When we talk about what we *need*, we're having a serious conversation: a need is different from just wanting or liking something; a *need* means it's really important for your development.

But there's a tendency to get too practical here. We feel we have to say that our actual needs (the things we really, really require) have to be very simple – food, water, oxygen (thanks plants), a roof over our heads, a few years of education. And it is terrible that not everyone in the world gets enough of even these basic things.

But you might also genuinely need some less practical things. You might properly need the chance to be creative through art or to study the oboe with a very good teacher or to play your favourite sport or to have long conversations with someone who has explored the world or who has made a really interesting career for themselves.

You could call these the 'CO_2 needs': the needs you might have that no one expected but which are essential to you.

Have a think about your CO_2 needs: what might yours be?

What do you love that others might be able to help you with?

What fears do you have around asking for help from others?

If someone could give you an opportunity that would allow you to explore what you really believe in, what might it be?

What might you be able to offer to other people?

Having a need isn't the same as having it met. But if you understand your needs, you can (maybe) get a little bit braver and a little bit more inventive about seeking out the help and friendships that would benefit you.

California, USA, 1920s

What's So Great About the Big Bang?

One of the strangest – and grandest – questions anyone can ask is:

Where did everything come from?

Not just humans or the Earth – but *everything!* Was the universe just always there? For infinity? So, if you went back a trillion years, or a trillion trillion, or a trillion times *that*, would the universe still have been there? That seems weird because the idea that the universe *never* started is even more baffling than the already mind-bending question: how did it start?

In the past, people believed that God – or the gods – had created the universe. But how God or the gods got there, no one could say. And how they might have been able to make planets and stars from nothing couldn't be explained.

It was really only in the early 20th century that scientists began to get a clue – not even a full answer, but a clue – about how planets and stars could have been made from nothing.

Once astronomers were able to make really powerful telescopes that could see far beyond our galaxy to many millions of more distant ones, they started to notice something very odd. The discovery was made in 1929 by American astronomer Edwin Hubble.

Using the powerful Hooker telescope at Mount Wilson Observatory in California, Hubble's observations confirmed that all galaxies are moving away from each other at ultra-high speed. The universe is expanding, and that suggests that it used to be smaller. The further back in time you go, the smaller it must have been. And if you go back far enough, it would just have been the size of a pinhead, then less and less until ... what? It wasn't there at all?

That sounds so impossible. But there were some other clues as well. One was to do with the structure of atoms. Do you remember what we found out about atoms on pages 102–107 ? Atoms are mostly made up of empty space, with a tiny core surrounded by miniscule electrons. What if you squashed the cores together? Then you could pack a whole lot of matter into a very small space, making it incredibly dense. But even the core of an atom, composed of protons and neutrons, is almost entirely empty. The protons and neutrons are just made up of tiny quarks. So, if you could squeeze all those indescribably minute quarks together, you could get all the matter in the cosmos into the tiniest imaginable space.

The idea, then, is that around 13.8 billion years ago, at the very start of our universe, all the particles that make up all the atoms that exist today – and the entire universe – were packed together in an incredibly small, hot and dense single point. They then exploded and expanded at a tremendous rate – and this was the Big Bang with which our universe started. We know this much is true. We don't yet know anything at all about why it happened or what came before, if anything did.

This is a puzzling, but very grand story. All the numbers in it are insanely big, or insanely small. The universe was so small; it became so vast; it happened so long ago; the scale of the explosion was so enormous...

If you really try to get your head round it (none of us can, really, but we can try), something slightly odd and possibly rather wonderful happens. You might find that you start to forget about yourself and your own worries.

In your mind, you are going over such an astonishing story that your own problems might start to feel less important. If the universe was writing an autobiography, neither you nor we would get a mention in the index. It would all be about the beginnings of atoms and how stars and planets were formed. The whole of human history takes up a very small part of cosmic history. There are 200 billion trillion stars (approximately), so what happens around our Sun isn't likely to get a special mention, unless maybe there's a tiny note on how pretty the rings of Saturn turned out to be.

It's a funny thought and it can make you feel very small and a bit strange: if the universe is so big and so old and we are by comparison a tiny, brief speck in history ... maybe our day-to-day worries are not so important after all.

Of course, you are important, but sometimes it is really helpful to have a big perspective – to help balance out our focus on smaller problems (when everything feels like it matters so much and it's hard to see past it).

What kinds of things do you worry about every day? Maybe a tricky science test, who won the race at sports day, who said what about whom or how big (or small) someone's home is.

These things might not really matter very much when you imagine the scale of the universe: we're one species, living on a small planet slightly in the suburbs (as it were) of an ordinary galaxy, at a moment that doesn't even count as the blink of an eye.

The sort of things we are worried about now, we probably won't be worried about for very long.

Try this exercise on the next page. Pick out one or two things that (even if just from time to time) worry you and make you feel a bit anxious. Then imagine trying to look back at them from next month, or next year, or twenty years, or fifty years ... or a thousand, a million, a billion ...

Are they getting smaller and smaller, until they are hardly there? It's a fascinating thing our minds can do. The point isn't that we shouldn't care about or deal with our worries or try to put things right. It's a bit different. It's that they are only a big deal right now.

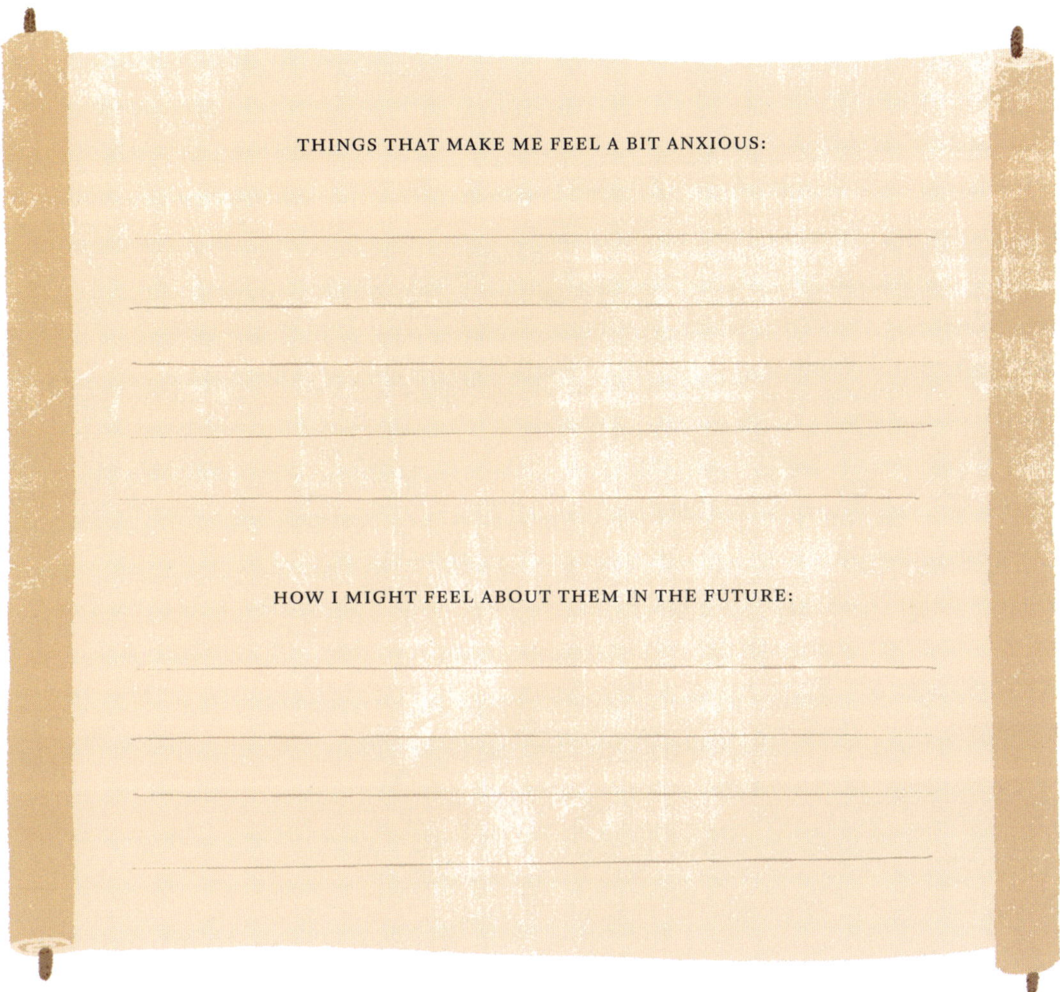

The chances are that in the future, you won't even remember the things that are worrying you now. We can deal best with our troubles when we feel calmer and clear-headed, rather than when we're in a panic, and sometimes a different perspective can help.

California, USA, 1960s-1970s

The Science of Waiting

In the 1970s, Professor Walter Mischel wanted to find out how good young children were at waiting for things they really wanted, so he designed a very simple experiment. The professor asked various preschool children to look at a marshmallow on a plate and then said: you are going to be left alone in this room for fifteen minutes. You can eat this marshmallow now, but if you wait until I come back, you can have two marshmallows instead.

This experiment was looking at something very basic about ourselves. Rather than trying to learn about how leaves make oxygen or what atoms are, these scientists were trying to understand how good we are at waiting for something better (and maybe also how much we like marshmallows).

What do you think happened in the experiment?

Would you *eat the marshmallow straight away or wait patiently for two?*

The professor found that most children actually did eat the marshmallow straight away. Some resisted for a while and then grabbed it. And only a few waited and got two. (If it turned out they didn't like marshmallows anyway, their behaviour wasn't included in the results.) The obvious conclusion was that children would rather take what they have right now, rather than wait for something better in the future.

It turns out to be a hugely important issue in our lives since – so often – we are faced with basically the same question: do you want something nice *now* or is it better to *defer gratification*, which is a frightfully clever way of saying 'have more nice things *later*'? For instance, do you get on with a school project straight away and have it all done well in time so you can relax, or do you have a fun weekend and end up doing it all in a rush at the end? If you are hungry, do you have a toasted sandwich or a plate of biscuits now or do you wait a quarter of an hour for dinner? Do you save money for one big thing that you really want, or do you spend it now on lots of smaller things?

Maybe it's reassuring to know that in the experiment, most children chose to eat the marshmallow. That's immediately rather nice because it shows you that when you don't want to wait, it's not because you are unusually impatient or make bad choices, but because you are like most other people. It's completely normal for human beings to do something fun straight away and avoid doing something more difficult, even if that difficult thing is going to bring a reward in the future.

But the experiment went on to track the later lives of the children, and it found some interesting results: it turned out that some of the children who waited had more academic success later on. That makes quite a lot of sense: it just means that in general they were good at doing all the necessary preparation in advance. This seems to conclude that in some ways it is better to be self-controlled, patient and to put off enjoyment for the future – *and* that hardly anyone is like this. Thanks a lot, Professor!

However, the marshmallow experiment was flawed. There were a lot of factors that weren't thought about, including the fact that children were only involved in it once, so they didn't get the chance to learn. Suppose you do the experiment once and take the marshmallow, but then you feel disappointed when the professor comes back in with two and won't give them to you. What would you do if you could take the test again? Would you choose differently? What about the third, or the twentieth time? We're pretty sure that eventually you might choose to wait for the reward. And maybe this is what science is really telling us: we need to practise things.

A bit later, scientists got very interested in exactly this: how do we learn to get strong in our mind? The brain is a bit like a muscle: it gets stronger the more you use it. If you make yourself do something a little tricky a few times, it quickly starts to feel much easier. This seems like a tiny thing but it's maybe one of the biggest issues in life.

A really good method to test this is to start with the tiniest possible change. Suppose you are afraid of heights. Instead of climbing to the top of a ladder and seeing how you feel ('terrified!'), you stand on a single sheet of paper, raising you a fabulous 0.2 mm above the ground. How do you feel? Fantastic? Great – come back tomorrow. Then you move up to 2 mm and then ten and twenty and so on. You keep going very, very gradually and your brain adjusts with equal slowness. Eventually you can stand on a ladder: it might take a while, but you can do it.

Maybe the marshmallow experiment was flawed because it started with something too difficult, and it wasn't repeated. If it started with 'don't touch this boring paperclip and I'll give you two marshmallows in eleven seconds', more children would have probably waited. If it had started easy and then became harder, we'd all have learned along the way. It's just that we haven't practised enough to develop the waiting skills we need.

Despite this, we've still learnt a lot from this experiment. We can see that maybe most people are naturally inclined not to wait for something better and do the easy thing first, but that we can train ourselves to behave differently if we choose to.

What do you tend to put off? Is there anything you are avoiding? What specific thing are you afraid of?

What's the least frightening version of this (working for 2 minutes, getting into the water for 5 seconds ...)?

Can you remember a time when you did try something you felt a little anxious about? Did you surprise yourself by doing it? How did you feel afterwards?

Your Imagination, Today

Could You Be Friends With an AI Bot?

In the middle of the 20th century, one of the founding figures of modern computing – a mathematician and computer scientist called Alan Turing – developed a test that would tell us when a machine was starting to show intelligent behaviour. Imagine, he said, you are just sending and receiving messages; could a robot, or at least an Artificial Intelligence (AI) program, mimic a human?

The test involved a human evaluator having a conversation through a text-based interface with another human and then with a computer. The evaluator interacted with both and asked them questions. If the evaluator couldn't tell which was the human and which was the computer, then the computer was deemed to be mimicking humans.

It's rather an interesting test, because it's not asking how obviously *clever* AI can get, but whether it can be like a human. Think about playing chess online: it's essentially a way of sending messages (your moves) and getting replies (your opponent's moves). But what often gives away that you are playing against a computer is precisely that the reply-moves are too good and too fast. And in fact, this is part of how cheating is detected.

In some ways, you might think AI has already passed (or is in the process of passing) the Turing Test. Suppose you're browsing for a film to watch; many streaming services use AI to determine which shows they should recommend to you based on what you've previously watched. Or perhaps you use voice assistants on your smart devices at home; both use AI to understand and react to your voice.

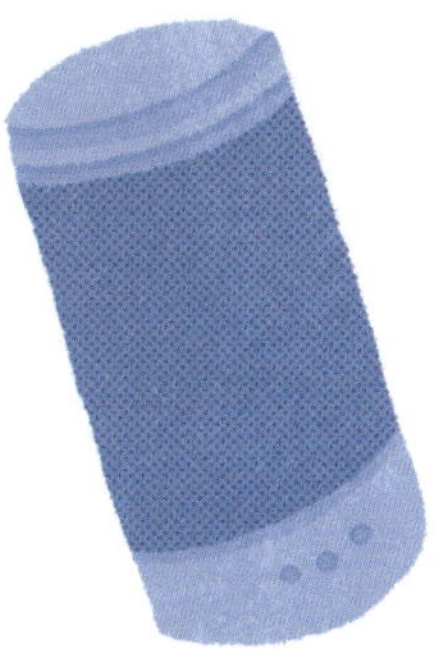

But actually, Turing suggested that the test could be more difficult. Instead of asking your voice assistant to play a certain song, suppose you want to *discuss* your favourite music. (Turing liked poetry so he imagined asking AI about poetry.) You could imagine doing the same with a book or a film. You'd want to know *what* they liked (or didn't) about it and you'd want them to explain *why*.

This is a very crucial moment in thinking. If you ask an AI these sorts of questions, it could probably give some quite convincing answers: it might say the film was great because there was a lot of action, or the song was super because the beat was regular. Another human would, maybe, give answers like these too. But those answers don't really convey any real feelings or deeper insights about the film or song.

A better version of the test, we'd suggest, is that you have to really *like* the interaction. You'd have to come away from the discussion thinking things like: that was extremely interesting, I'd never thought about those things before, and yes, they really got what I love about that line or that scene, only I'd not been able to put it into words before.

We'll know we have made great progress in programming AI when, after a few days of interaction, you feel the two of you could actually be very good friends.

And, oddly, the key thing for this test isn't directly to do with programming at all; it's to do with understanding what good friendship is. It's asking what would a robot or AI bot need to be able to do to pass a friendship test?

Think about friends for a moment. There are acquaintances – people you rather like but don't actually know that well. They may be fun to be around, but you can't be open and honest with them about who you really are.

Then there are the rarer people with whom you can be truly yourself: those who will properly listen to and take on board the complexity of what it's like to be you. They like you for who you are because they have an equally complex secret self to reveal – especially to you. They are your true friends and the kind of thing that AI can't replicate, yet.

What's the difference between a proper friend and someone you just quite like?

What does a good friend do?

What does a good friend NOT do?

How do you become friends with someone?

These are huge, lifelong questions, and the idea isn't that you'll have a perfect answer right now, but that you are developing your ideas on this topic – since deep friendship can be very important in our lives, but also much more rare than it ideally should be.

And so finally you can ask:

Could AI ever become a genuinely good friend?

This is a really pivotal moment for the future. We may still be overly impressed by what technology can currently do for us, but can it ever replicate true friendship?

In the long term there's no reason to think that technology could not rise to such a challenge. We are physical creatures; our carbon-based brains support everything we think and feel, and there's no logical reason why something made of silicone and plastic couldn't, if programmed the right way, attain a similar level of nuance and depth. But would it really be the same? Perhaps time will tell ...

A great task for the future – which might fall to you – will be to say, 'we're not there yet'.

Who Knows Where, Who Knows When

What Might Aliens Be Like?

Over the last few thousand years, we've gone from wondering how big the Earth is to discovering that the universe is probably filled with an unimaginably large number of planets – some of which are bound to be similar to ours or at least hospitable to intelligent life.

However, with our current technology, there's no way we could possibly reach them. The distances are so massive that it would take our fastest rocket more than 73,000 years to reach even our closest neighbouring star (apart from our Sun), Proxima Centauri. So, the most likely chance of direct contact is if they come to us. Let's imagine they are on their way and going to arrive pretty soon. What should we expect?

The spaceship lands, a door opens and something or someone comes out. Here's a question for you:

What do they look like? Could you do a drawing of them?

But apart from what they look like, there are more serious issues to consider: what do they want? Why are they here? What are they going to do? Are they kind or mean? Are they curious about us, or are they angry with us and looking to take over our planet? Take a bit of time to imagine their attitude. They've come all this way – how do they feel about us humans?

Many people might be quite excited about the idea of alien visitors; however, a lot of people worry that aliens would be hostile to us. At the end of the 19th century, there was a very successful book called *The War of the Worlds* by H.G. Wells. It imagined huge metal ships containing unseen aliens arriving from outer space. They slowly start to destroy all the cities, and no human weapons can stop them. Maybe the aliens want to steal our minerals, like copper or tin; maybe they think we're a threat. This broad idea has been repeated in countless other books and films.

But these ideas don't actually make a great deal of sense. The reason is that only a very, very advanced civilisation would ever be able to get here. It's hugely difficult to travel between different star systems. The aliens' technology would have to be incredibly sophisticated. So any civilisation that could reach us couldn't possibly need anything from us, nor could they be in any way threatened by us. We are totally incapable of reaching them or harming them in any way.

Another idea that has emerged is that if the arriving aliens are so sophisticated, perhaps they won't even notice we are here. They might confuse us with microbes; they won't mean to do us any harm, but they might wipe us out by accident (much like how you kill millions of bacteria when you wash your hands). But, again, this seems highly unlikely. Of course, we'll be much less advanced than them. They would know perfectly well the difference between microbes and us.

In fact, they'd be more likely to see us as the equivalent of babies, who know basically nothing compared to adults and need protecting. Adults are very conscious that to help a baby you must interact with the baby's needs. You don't say, 'Here's a book on advanced maths'; instead, you sing them songs and smile. We think that a highly intelligent civilisation that reached here would be likely to understand us – and our needs – very well.

Finally, there's a third theme that sometimes gets suggested: if aliens arrived here, they'd be *angry* with us. They would see our wars and our mistreatment of animals through hunting and the high carbon dioxide levels in the atmosphere. They'd look at us and shudder with disapproval and put a stop to us and the harm we do. This is very unlikely. A civilisation capable of getting here would probably have no trouble whatever in solving our problems. They would show us (in five seconds) how to extract excess carbon dioxide from the atmosphere. They would teach us how to restructure our economy and rethink our ideas. They could impose peace on the world with ease.

Deep down, the discussion of aliens isn't really about aliens at all. None of us has the slightest idea what they might actually be like. But how we imagine them and how we think they might behave says quite a lot about our own personality and worldview.

What we're talking about here is something called *projection*: the way your mind *imagines* what other people are like, even though you don't actually *know,* because of your own feelings and experiences.

People might imagine hostile aliens not because that's probable, but because they fear new or unknown things – or because they see how badly humans treat each other sometimes.

Projection is everywhere. We don't know most of the people we encounter, and yet we project ideas onto them about what they might be like. Quite often our picture of another person isn't really about them at all – it's about us. If we feel hostile towards strangers, we imagine strangers feel hostile towards us. If we imagine that aliens would be angry about the state of our world, maybe that's because we feel angry or upset about it ourselves.

THE FUTURE OF SCIENCE

What Will Scientists Find Out Next?

People in the past were often terrible at guessing where science would go next. They usually imagined the future in terms of more of what they already knew. In ancient times, people got excited about building towers. They might have imagined that in the future science would work out how to build a tower that could reach the Moon. It wouldn't have occurred to them then that we might use rockets instead.

Or, in the 1960s, when jet planes were the new big thing, many people thought the future would involve lots of jet engines. Thanks to science, they imagined that lucky children of the 21st century would all have jet packs and fly to school. And you know how that turned out ...

Because today we have lots of amazing technology, many people imagine a future filled with even more technology. But these pictures of future science might turn out to be just as wrong as the image of you and your classmates skilfully managing your morning descent into the school landing ground.

The problem with how people *tend* to imagine the future of science is that they get excited by things that sound cool and fun but are ultimately not the most useful things. Building a tower to the Moon *sounded* exciting but is actually a rather flawed idea. There are easier ways to get there – and not everyone needs to visit the Moon.

Flying to school *sounded* brilliant, but *how* you get to school is actually almost always a fairly minor issue in your life in comparison to what happens once you are there. Spending your entire life online *sounds* futuristic but is it your best picture of the life you actually want?

So, let's think about a future for science that might really be fantastic and help us in big and lovely ways.

Here's our wish list:

I. THE SCIENCE OF HAPPINESS

One reason for improvement in many areas is to make people happier. But what is a happy life? What actually makes a life happier? We're still a bit away from solving this problem, but a few ideas are falling into place.

Having a sense of being loved may be one of the most important factors in what makes a human being happy and fulfilled. You would think, then, that this would be a main focus of pretty much all our efforts. But it's not. Instead, the world is focused on making material things, like cool T-shirts and expensive trainers, which might only bring temporary joy and not lasting happiness.

Another big theme is that people are usually happier when they feel they are in a job that really suits them. But as yet, we've collectively devoted almost no effort to working out what this actually means or how to bring it about.

We could imagine a future science that puts more effort into working out in great detail what we need to do now (in small and big ways) to actually make ourselves happier and more content in our lives.

Imagine you are a scientist working on *The Great Theory of Happiness* project – and you've just been given a lot of funding. What sorts of problems would you like to solve?

II. AI THAT REALLY HELPS US

Science and technology are always looking for ways to solve problems and make life a little bit easier. They invented dishwashers because washing up by hand can be a bit boring, and they invented sat nav because it makes it easier for us to find our way around. But there are many other sorts of problems that technology hasn't properly addressed yet.

Imagine your phone – or a small implant in your arm – could track if you were getting too annoyed with someone and send you a message like, 'Now might be a good time to say sorry'. Or maybe it could detect if you weren't properly understanding what someone was saying, and prompt you to ask a thoughtful question.

It would take a lot of progress in science to do this. Scientists would have to study the brain in great detail to identify the tell-tale signs of getting annoyed for a not very good reason or of not understanding when you don't consciously realise you aren't understanding. There would surely be highly complicated patterns of brain activity that could be identified and tracked when we are in these situations. With this knowledge, AI could give you really good advice, just at the moment when you need it.

And the advice could be tailored just to suit you. Maybe you want it to sound like a joke, or be delivered in Granny's voice.

You could imagine an AI that understands how to help you. If it detected that you were half wishing you could stop watching videos, but also half desperate to keep watching them, it might suggest that you take a little break. If you were a bit upset by something mean another person said to you, it would know how to calm you down and cheer you up. And if you were about to send a mean message (we all feel the temptation sometimes), it might say, in the voice of a really good friend, 'I know how you feel, but are you sure you really want to send that?'

What would you ideally like AI to help you with?

III. AN APP TO HELP 'TRANSLATE' OTHER PEOPLE

It's very useful to have an app that can instantly translate foreign words into your own language. But a language barrier is just one of the ways you can find it difficult to make sense of other people. Wouldn't it be useful if you had an app to help you understand them?

Imagine someone is always boasting. They keep saying how great they are, and what great things they have. It can be rather irritating and make you feel bad in comparison. But what might the translation app reveal? It might tell you that what that person is really saying is, 'I worry that people won't like me, so I have to keep on stressing all the ways I'm special to make friends'.

Or suppose someone keeps being mean to others, saying things like, 'Your hair looks silly' or 'You are rubbish at sports; you're a loser'. They are acting like a bully. Let's ask the app what this person might *really* be trying to express: 'My dad and my older cousin are always telling me that I'm useless. I'm frightened of them, which makes me feel sad and lonely. The only way I know how to communicate is by being mean.'

Or what about someone who is very shy? They hardly even say hello, and if they do, it's in a very quiet voice. Here's how the app might translate their mumbled words: 'I'm scared. I'd actually love to be friends with you.

Please keep trying gently and don't give up on me. Once you get to know me, you'll find I have lots of interesting ideas.'

Or perhaps you see someone in a supermarket restocking the shelves, and when Mum says, 'I'm looking for halogen light bulbs' they just reply, 'Third aisle'.

But the app might say 'third aisle' actually means: 'Hi, I'm working here part-time and also studying for a degree in marine biology. I love playing basketball with my friends. I'd really like to talk to you more, but my manager is always checking how much work I've done. By the way, the halogen bulbs are in the third aisle; so lovely to meet you'.

Sometimes, with people, what is really going on is a lot more interesting – and a lot nicer – than it appears.

Science has become very good at detecting a lot of things we can't see: volcanoes deep under the ocean, the existence of atoms, or light from incredibly distant stars, which is too faint for our own eyes to perceive. Yet, despite these discoveries, the hardest thing to detect might be the most important of all: what's actually going on in the minds of others.

Science and Myth

Remember, right at the beginning of the book, we were talking about how ancient societies created stories – some of the grandest and most beautiful ever told – about how the world began and how nature worked? They were being very clever and creative, given their limited knowledge. They *couldn't* have known what we know now: it took centuries of effort, thinking, experimentation, and, sometimes, luck for scientists to understand how things work. And they're still figuring lots of things out today!

But imagine how hard it must have been to move away from myths and ideas that had been around for centuries. Imagine you grow up being told that the stars are the spirits of your ancestors, looking down at you from the sky with love. When you see them at night, you feel safe. Then science comes along and says, 'Sorry, actually we've discovered that stars are actually giant balls of hot gas very, very far away'.

What science says is true, but what does it mean for myths and all the deep, wonderful things that people have believed for centuries? What about the rainbow being a sign that the gods are happy, or the sacred tree that protects the tribe? Are they just nice stories that we should ignore? Absolutely not! Myths and stories are really important, but for quite different reasons.

OK, so thinking the stars are the spirits of your ancestors isn't really a very scientific way of thinking about stars. But the stars are millions (sometimes billions) of years old. This means that the same stars you see today were also seen by your ancestors. Isn't that amazing? Myths and stories are a really good way of caring about, and feeling loyal and connected to, those who lived before you. An idea can be doing something very important – even though there are other practical explanations.

You could say your ancestors are *like* the stars (always there, always out of reach); seeing a rainbow might make you *feel* happy and that's important. Or the tree can be a *symbol* of continuity and regeneration: you want your tribe to survive as the tree has; you want every difficult time (like winter) to be followed by regeneration (like spring). Just because these stories are made up, doesn't mean they hold no meaning or importance.

Teaching People About Science

One of the tricky things about science is that sometimes the explanations it presents do not line up with what we might want. Some people reject science because the results it comes up with are *inconvenient* and *annoying* to them. They don't *like* what science is saying, so they say it's *not true*.

Or people do not quite understand what science is telling them. The explanations about climate change or the latest technology can be confusing and long-winded. Scientists use big, complicated words, and in the end, the person gives up and ignores the latest scientific discovery. That sort of response is deeply understandable. So, what happens is that important things science wants to say end up not reaching people – or getting rejected by a lot of people.

So, what to do? Actually, the answer has to do with something you probably know a lot about:

What makes a good teacher?

A good teacher knows perfectly well when an idea is difficult to grasp or when it might be upsetting. So, they're careful in how they present it. They show you, in lots of ways, that they like and respect you; they're interested in what you think and why. They make learning fun. They help you feel brave. They would never make you feel bad for not understanding something.

Science discovers how things are; but accepting and dealing with how things are is another matter for us as humans. So, we don't just need scientists; we need teachers too, to show us non-scientists what it all means, in ways we can understand. There are some people who think, 'The world is in crisis, the icebergs are melting; I must study climate change'. But the problem isn't that we lack information. The challenge is that it's hard for a lot of people – who lead busy lives and have other things to worry about – to pay proper attention. We think it's the scientists who are doing the crucial work; after all, the news always says, 'Scientists have discovered that ...'. But maybe it's the teachers, really, who are doing the crucial work: helping people to understand and accept the complicated truth.

Technology and science often give us remarkable powers, but we don't always use them wisely. For instance, it is truly amazing that we can communicate with practically everyone on the planet at the touch of a screen. But, often this immense, astonishing power is used for things that are not at all helpful. There are many downsides to being connected through the internet and social media, including addiction, frustration, hatred and (sometimes) the sharing of very bad ideas.

It is incredible that we have discovered a huge amount about atoms, but this knowledge has also led to the development of deadly bombs, so rules have had to be put in place to stop people from building them.

You could say that science is like a very powerful tool – it can be used for a lot of different things. What it's used for depends on *who* is using it, and that means us – humans. A sharp knife is really useful if you want to slice an apple or dice a carrot, but it can also be dangerous if you use it carelessly. That's why we know you have to be rather sensible and grown up before handling one. We can say the same about science. Science gives us power, but maybe a lot of the time we're not – collectively – wise enough to use that power very well.

Science, you could say, is only as good or bad as the community that uses it. It can be used for wonderful or dangerous things, much like a sharp knife. In an ideal world, new technology and tools would be developed by responsible, intelligent people and would only be shared with those who are kind enough, and wise enough, to use them well.

This has always been the challenge. Remember on pages 40–45, we were talking about the invention of bronze, which could be used to make wonderful ornaments but also swords. At the time, it gave whoever had it an immense advantage. Suppose bronze had been developed and only used by people who wanted to keep the peace. They could have used their superiority to make things much better for everyone. But bronze very often fell into the hands of people who wanted to defeat their enemies and seize land.

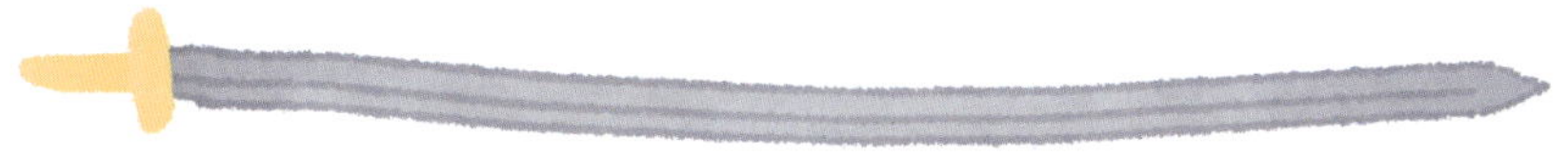

Or take – much later on – the invention of concrete. Concrete can be used to build the most lovely things, or very ugly things. Concrete itself doesn't decide – we do. It's the sharp knife all over again.

The coming decades and centuries will bring new science and technology, and increasing power. In twenty or forty years, we will have inventions that we can currently hardly imagine today. Who will discover these things? How will they be used? Will they help us become better and improve the world, or will they be used for selfish purposes and make it easier to do harm?

In the middle of the 20th century, a scientist and writer called C.P. Snow gave a lecture called 'The Two Cultures', which was later published. In it, he was frustrated about how people who were interested in the arts and poetry – what is beautiful and sad and tender – often knew little about science. And people who cared a lot about science tended to know very little about the arts and poetry.

It would be lovely to think that the people who will be at the centre of science in the future will also be thinking about life and what makes a good one. And that the people who have the most influence on what others think, like writers, influencers, business leaders and politicians, will also be knowledgeable about science.

We think what really matters is this:

Are enough people interested in science and (at the same time) wise enough to use science well?

We need people who are kind, who love nature, who want to be good friends, and who are interested in art, poetry and sport to also be interested in science, and vice versa.

Science doesn't decide what matters – that's up to us.

And, more importantly, it's up to you.

IMAGE CREDITS:

P. 56 Decorative motif from a Qur'an manuscript, Persian, 14th century. National Museum, Tehran. Photo © Roland & Sabrina Michaud/akg-images

P. 57 Blue dome of Shah Nematollah Vali Shrine, Mahan, Kerman province, Iran. Photo © Petr Kahanek/dreamstime.com

What are YOUR Big Ideas?

ALSO AVAILABLE FOR CHILDREN FROM THE SCHOOL OF LIFE

Big Ideas for Curious Minds

An introduction to philosophy

Children are, in many ways, born philosophers. Without prompting, they ask some of the largest questions: about time, mortality, happiness and the meaning of it all. Yet sadly, too often, this inborn curiosity is not developed and, with age, the questions fall away.

Big Ideas for Curious Minds is designed to harness children's spontaneous philosophical instinct and to develop it through introductions to some of the most vibrant and essential philosophical ideas of history. The book takes us to meet leading figures of philosophy from around the world and from all eras – and shows us how their ideas continue to matter.

ISBN: 978-1-9997471-4-5

Big Ideas from History

A history of the world for you

The present can loom very large in a child's mind: all the challenges of the modern world can feel overwhelming and, at times, dispiriting. *Big Ideas from History* is an immense story of what has happened through time, from the beginnings of the universe to now, that speaks personally and constructively to a growing mind.

The book encourages children to think about how and why they experience the world as they do and offers a helpful perspective by placing their thoughts and feelings in the context of our history. What might the dinosaurs or the Ancient Egyptians, the Aztec warriors or the Enlightenment thinkers of the 18th century, tell us that could be interesting and useful to hear now? The book also looks to the future and asks the reader to imagine a world they would like to live in. It is a thoughtful and inspiring introduction to the world around us, which encourages the child to engage with themselves and others through history.

ISBN: 978-1-912891-80-1

ALSO AVAILABLE FOR CHILDREN FROM THE SCHOOL OF LIFE

Big Ideas from Literature

How books can change your world

From an early age, we tend to be told that books matter, but very rarely are we properly allowed to examine why – and therefore we can miss out on a genuine engagement with books. *Big Ideas from Literature* dares to ask the obvious but crucial questions about the whole business of reading: What is reading really for? What are stories trying to do for us? Why should we care?

In a tone that's engaging and playful, we're shown how books help us to grow, why we cry about the fate of certain characters and how to read for genuine pleasure rather than to please a teacher or parent. Along the way, we learn about the history of literature and about some of the many fascinating books from around the world we might enjoy.

Always, the underlying concern is to foster a love of reading, while appreciating that this might require us to first bluntly question why we should even bother. *Big Ideas from Literature* helps us with the greatest challenge we can ever have around books: how to make them into our true friends.

ISBN: 978-1-915087-48-5

ALSO AVAILABLE FOR CHILDREN FROM THE SCHOOL OF LIFE

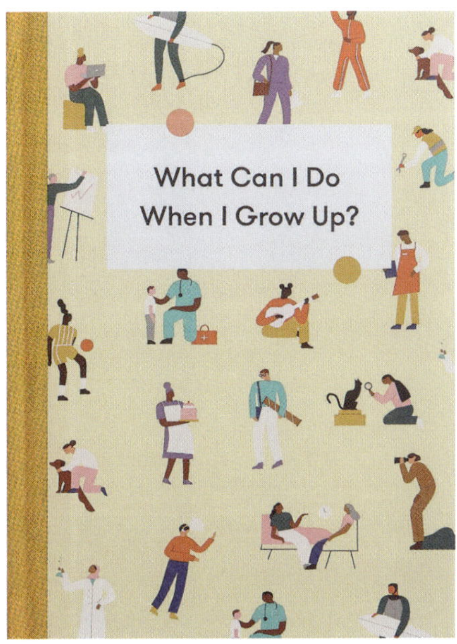

What Can I Do When I Grow Up?

A young person's guide to careers, money – and the future

Have you ever felt confused, scared or even a little annoyed when an adult has asked, as if it were the most normal thing in the world: what do you want to do when you grow up? If so, you are not alone. Knowing what you want to do with your life is one of the hardest questions you will ever have to answer and it's one that most adults are still grappling with ...

What Can I Do When I Grow Up? is a book about the world of work written expressly for young people. It takes us on a journey around the most essential questions within the topic, such as: *how can I discover my passions? What should a 'good' job involve? How much money should I make? How does the economy work?*

The result is a book that will spark exceptionally fruitful conversations and help you look forward to your work life with positivity and anticipation.

ISBN: 978-1-912891-20-7

THE SCHOOL OF LIFE

The School of Life is a global organisation helping people lead more fulfilled lives. It is a resource for helping us understand ourselves, for improving our relationships, our careers and our social lives – as well as for helping us find calm and get more out of our leisure hours.

We do this through films, workshops, books and gifts – and provide a warm and supportive community. You can find us online, in stores and in welcoming spaces around the globe.

www.theschooloflife.com